Table of Contents

Foreward

Life is not easy.

Each and everyone of us faces our own unique challenges and yet we are all connected in various ways, even if it is simply in realizing that we are not alone in this world and we can learn from the experiences of others.

A crucial key to finding happiness in life is in the awareness that we can all exercise more control over our destiny using the power of our own mind. Sometimes it's easy to accept a victim mindset, feeling powerless to deal with what life brings, yet when one discovers that they have the ability to take back control of their emotions, their choices and decisions in life improve, and their very destiny shifts as a result of new thinking.

Faulty thinking and irrational behavior can be habitual, due to erroneous programming of the subconscious mind throughout life to this point. Change happens only when a person wants and is willing to visualize life differently. Anthony Gitch, through his courage in writing this book and sharing his personal story, provides the tools for transformational change and he leads the reader forward as he lays out exactly how to step away from victimhood and codependency, and the endless and needless suffering of life in that mindset. He shows you how to make the positive shift that leads to that new you, which is guaranteed to emerge, as you decide to allow.

Anger, codependency and pessimism are all easily overcome with the tools and insights presented by Anthony. Discover in these pages how the mind works as you explore four core survival archetypes, allowing your heightened awareness of what is going on in your life now, in the present moment, so you can see your path forward based on your own intentions.

As you read this book I wonder at what point you begin to realize you are standing on the shoulders of a giant, someone courageous enough to share his life's experience so that you may ease some of the burdens in your own life.

The quality of your life is, in large part, entirely up to you moving forward from today. I urge you to muster the same courage that Anthony has shown in this book and take a bold step. In a tough love style, this book presents a clear path forward and for many will be like holding a mirror up to one's life.

The good news is no matter your circumstances, this book provides both empowerment and hope. You can put a stop to the constant struggle as you connect with your true self, feeling more worthy and certainly 'perfect enough' to do anything you put your mind to doing. You deserve to be happier and live an abundant, joyful life.

It's time to go on a very important journey now, with Anthony, and take charge! Anthony is with you through every page of this book, there to help you navigate even the most treacherous of emotional storms.

As the famous last stanza of William Henley's poem, Invictus, so vividly states:

It matters not how strait the gate,

How charged with punishments the scroll,

I am the master of my fate:

I am the captain of my soul.

Take charge, captain!

Dr. Richard Nongard

A Hero's Journey

Heroes are made in the hour of defeat. Success is, therefore, well described as a series of glorious defeats.

— Mahatma Gandhi

Truth Talk

You are now on notice, you no longer have an excuse to whine, complain, or blame anyone for the unpleasant situations you find yourself in. It is time to buck up and take responsibility for your happiness. I tell every single client on their first visit with me the same thing I am going to share with you now. I want you to be prepared to experience major shifts in your reality and perceptions, and I want you to be prepared—it will not always be a comfortable journey.

It is my job to teach you how to destroy the unhealthy foundations of belief that you've built your problems on. The rug of reality you stand on will be pulled from under your feet, and so you have a choice: Grip tightly to that which has not been working for you, your story—and we know it hasn't been working for you, otherwise you wouldn't be reading or listening to this book—or stop making up excuses, stop your whining, blaming, complaining, being angry all the time, and learn to take responsibility for your life so that you can achieve the happiness you desire.

The next thing I make sure clients understand on that first visit is that no one can make you change. No one can do the work for you. If you find yourself coming up with reasons, excuses, validations, or whatever you want to call them for not doing what is suggested, then don't bother. Really, why waste your time and add yet another failed, half assed attempt to the list you're attempting to burn? I have clients who say that they are willing to do whatever it takes to be happy—right up until I actually give them something to do. All of a sudden, a flood of reasons are released, like I don't have the time, I have to do this or that with the kids or for work. Listen, if you want to change, you can, but you have to make the time to make it happen. You did not get to where you are overnight, so do not expect to become who you want to be overnight.

If you are reading this book, you have one or all of these things going on. You get angry easily, sometimes without provocation. You attempt to control any and all situations you can. You regularly compare your life to the lives others, and, for whatever reason, it seems like no matter what you do, you just can't seem to get ahead. You are on antidepressants or have been

2

diagnosed as depressed or suffering from anxiety, have weight issues, addiction issues, or life just doesn't seem fair and your flipping tired of standing on the sidelines waiting, hoping for something to change. You're just waiting to catch that one big break. I am not saying that life is horrible for you, but you're looking for something more, and you are tired of the constant struggle that is your day to day existence.

However unjust or unfair you think it is, it seems as if everyone else out there gets what they want, except you. Even those who appear not to apply themselves seem to be able to climb the ladder of success and get what they want. Then there are the ones who are born with a silver spoon in their mouth. They are the worst, right? Must be nice when mommy and daddy will bail you out all the time. Shoot, it would be nice if a family member or longtime friend believed in you even a little bit. My God, if anyone would believe in even one of the ideas you've had, things would be so much different.

If these are the kind of thoughts or feelings that you have on a regular basis, or even semi regularly, then you are ultimately destroying any chance you have at ever being really happy. You see, these thoughtforms create a negative loop in your mind, increasing anxiety, stress, judgement, envy, and feelings of inadequacy. Left unchecked and running wild in the untrained mind, these thought patterns lead to frustration, anger, depression, and self-hate. You start to only see the bad things about your life and yourself. The wins fade away, not because they don't exist but because you hold yourself to such high standards that nothing is ever good enough for you. The praise from other people feels fake, and you start to resent them for thinking that you're stupid enough to be manipulated by their insincerity. Your radar is finely tuned to everyone else's trickery, and your defenses deploy at mach speed, fully armed and ready to attack, sometimes without provocation. Have you ever considered how many opportunities have been lost to friendly fire?

You have spent day after day and year after year working to catch that one big break. To find the partner of your dreams and have it all just fall into place. I mean, you see it happen to people all the time, right? If this is your belief, then you have fallen victim to a societal trap or a belief within the collective consciousness that happiness depends on something outside of yourself.

Here is the problem with hoping to catch a break or find something "out there" or outside of yourself to fulfill something "in here" or within you. Any time you're looking to catch something, it will do what is natural to all things being hunted or pursued—it will run, and it will do whatever it can to evade you. It doesn't matter if it is financial success, the perfect partner, or any other part of the life you dream about having. As long as you continue hunting or searching for "it," "It" will never appear because "It" is always changing. You are in a constant state of mutation, of growth, and as you grow and learn, your needs, wants, and desires grow with you. They begin to change, but this is not a phenomena that you feel or are able recognize on a conscious level because it so subtle and happens below your awareness. The pain caused by this process is most noticeable when you do not have clearly defined goals because you inevitably get sidetracked or loose site of the original intent You may even have had the experience when you have thought that you'd finally caught your big break only to come to the realization

4

that the perfect partner was not so perfect after all. When all was said and done, you were still unsatisfied, and you still did not have the life you wanted, or you don't feel the sense of accomplishment that you expected to feel and that you see other people feel.

Smack of reality here. You will never experience the kind of anger, joy, laughter, sadness, or anything else that you see others experience, period. Why? Because when it comes right down to the nitty gritty of things, you have no way to know what they are experiencing. You cannot be in their head.

Most people who are in a highly emotional state couldn't tell you what they are feeling in the moment. But you, like most people, think because the outside expression looks all nice that the interior is as well organized. The bigger point here is why would you want to experience reality from their point of view? How do you know that what they are expressing as joy is what you consider to be joy? Better yet, think about how others look at you when you express what you call anger, to some of your friends and family, you turn into a raging psycho over what they may consider a minor infraction. So, unplug from the idea that you want to experience life the way others do. Otherwise, you may get a prize that you never wanted.

I find this poem to be quite fitting when it comes to releasing yourself from the act of judging and comparing and begin moving into acceptance. I do not know who this is attributed to, but it was shared with me on the start of my journey and remains on my refrigerator door to this day.

Different Drummer

If I do not want what you want, please try not to tell me that my want is wrong.

Or if I believe other than you, at least pause before you correct my view.

Or if my emotion is less than yours, or more, given the same circumstances, try not to ask me to feel more strongly or weakly.

Or yet if I act, or fail to act, in the manner of your design for action, let me be.

I do not, for the moment at least, ask you to understand me.

That will come only when you are willing to give up changing me into a copy of you.

I may be your spouse, your parent, your child, your friend, or your colleague.

If you will allow me any of my own wants, or emotions, or beliefs, or actions, then you open yourself so that someday, these ways of mine might not seem so wrong and might finally appear to you as right — for me.

To put up with me is the first step to understanding me.

Not that you embrace my ways as right for you, but you are no longer irritated or disappointed with me for my seeming waywardness.

And in understanding me, you might come to prize my differences from you, and, far from seeking to change me, preserve and even nurture those differences.

By constantly judging others and comparing yourself to their perceived accomplishments, you limit your own possibilities. You also limit yourself to the capacity of those who you surround yourself with, and the danger here is that other people do not want what you want, and they cannot magically see the world with your eyes to understand your wants.

True to Yourself

Let me give you an example of how we create self-doubt and suffering with something as simple as home ownership. When I was growing up, my parents owned their home, and, just like all the other kids around us, my siblings and I were taught that the American dream includes homeownership. More to the point, society as a whole views home ownership as a sign of success or a rite of passage as it were into adult hood. At the time of this book, I am in my early 50's, and I have never owned my own home. For years, I beat myself up and thought of myself as a failure for not owning a home because my older sister and her husband have always had a lovely home, and my brother and his wife bought the house next door to the one we grew up in and had another built on a hillside overlooking one of the most beautiful spots on the Columbia River, so they are successful, right?

An untrained mind will hold to the believe that because one of those things is true—they own a home—the other thing must also be true; they are successful and happy. When in reality, one does not always lead to the other. In fact, when I ask most homeowners why they bought their home, they all say the same thing, "It's just what you're supposed to do." Where is the choice in that statement? There is none. When I really thought about it, I realized that I did not want to, and never have really wanted to, own a home. I do not want to be tied to the constant expenses and maintenance, and, more importantly, if I decide that I want to move, I can just get up and go. Until I unplugged from that repressive societal belief, I remained in a state of background suffering, never feeling like an equal or good enough.

Ugly Truth

Time to talk about the hard stuff. If you have ever physically abused someone, and you feel remorse for doing it, good. I am not here to help free you from the responsibility of your past actions. I will show you how to forgive yourself, but those feelings of shame and guilt for your misdeeds are there to remind you of what you are giving up and of your goal to be a better person. If you do not feel remorse, and instead, you feel justified for your past misdeed because of the other person's actions, then I suggest that you take a good hard look at yourself and decide if you are ready to be real and honest.

Are you ready to face the ugly truth and look at the damage you've done? Or do you want to spend the rest of your life trudging down the same ugly path you've been traveling? Again, it is time to buck up , take responsibility, and do what is needed to clean up your side of the street so that you can be free and happy. You are doing this for you. Your children, husband, wife, boyfriend, girlfriend, or any other person in your life, including your boss, will all benefit from you taking control. But your freedom from anger and your right to change remains at the core of your journey.

If you have been on the receiving end of abuse, and you made the choice to stay, regardless of the level of abuse, then you also have feelings of shame, guilt, resentment, and anger. You live with the knowledge that you allowed someone to treat you that way, and in doing so, diminished your self-esteem and self-worth. Please do recognize that I said it was your *choice* to stay. Does it hurt to hear that? Too bad! I told you at the start that it is time to set aside the whining, blaming, complaining, and anger. It is time to clear away the victim stories that you have been telling yourself and others for so long. You need to look at the damage you've done to yourself and those around you and grow from it. Otherwise, you remain a victim of your circumstances and nothing changes.

My Truth

If it seems that I have a view into your world, it is just a coincidence, and the coincidence is that I have walked your path. I know the pain that comes from being angry, defensive, codependent, and resentful. I think it's only fair that you understand why I feel so confident in my belief that you can attain the freedom and happiness you want. So confident, in fact, I actually make you that promise.

I understand what it feels like to be angry and to have a chip on your shoulder because I carried one around for years, and after being beat up multiple times as a child, and then again as an adult while involved in abusive relationships and because of the hate crimes I've been subjected to. I also know what it is like to feel enraged, out of control, and alone. More importantly, I know the path to freedom.

Here is just some of my old story, what I did to let go of my anger and what happened when I stopped whining, blaming, and complaining.

I have been the abused and I have also been the abuser.

I never got physical with my partners, but I would intentionally push them to their breaking point and then blame them for what they did. I would use their violence and mistreatment as currency with my friends, family, and coworkers. I would not become physical with them, but I assure you, the verbal abuse I would unleash was as damaging to the soul as a fist to the face or a knife in the belly.

I have lived with such extreme emotional ups and downs that I had my first heart attack like episode at the age of 26, a full 6 years after first seeking help to escape my anger and feelings of not being good enough. I was looking for any answers I could find as to why I was so angry all the time or why I would explode when women in power spoke down to me or anyone else. I couldn't keep a job, and a healthy relationship was out of the question. It was on my first visit to a counselor that I received a diagnosis of depression and a prescription for Wellbutrin. I was subsequently put on a variety of other antidepressants and antianxiety medications, including Prozac, Paxil, Xanax, and Zoloft, as well as a combination of those drugs. I was informed by one genius licensed mental health professional that my problems were caused by homosexuality and my inherent hatred toward my mother and other women. Absolutely worthless and laughable, but the medications did make the underlying dissatisfaction of life more tolerable, so I continued to take them without making any changes to how I was living my life. After all, the doctors never had suggestions or guidance about what I should do differently, or even that I do anything different, they just asked me what I thought I should do. I remember telling one of the many I sought help from that if I knew what to do different, I wouldn't need to be in their office asking them. I think that was my last traditional counseling session, and for years, I did what I could to keep the bad stuff at bay and only let people see the funny, happy guy who made everyone laugh.

Of course, the idea of keeping the constant feelings of disappointment and frustration at bay and under control was a farce. The negativity would come out as fits of self-pity that I used to manipulate people with. I could always point the finger at some circumstance or someone else in order to absolve myself from all responsibility. I couldn't see how my behavior was supporting the negative downward spiral that was my life.

However, I can look back now and see all the damage and hurt I inflicted on myself and the people around me, but I didn't know how to use the gift of hindsight.

This gift of hindsight allows you to see where you need to make changes in behavior and where you can improve on your ability to maintain staying in and with the present moment. My hindsight was broken, it didn't work correctly, or, rather, I didn't know how to use it properly. Instead of seeing what my part was in any situation and what I could do differently or how I could improve, I would only see where others had failed. Instead of

11

learning from hindsight, I manipulated it and wielded it as a weapon against anyone who suggested I take responsibility for the problems in my life.

I was the poster child for what I now call the VCCA or the Victims of Circumstance Club of America. I kept trying, but other people kept holding me back or getting in my way. There was always another reason behind whatever negative thing happened that had nothing to do with me, and nothing was my fault.

Here are four examples of beliefs that I held onto that ultimately kept me from succeeding. I will share the belief, and then I will share the reality, the real truth of the circumstance. I do this in some respect to show you that it is okay to be honest and vulnerable. My behavior in the past helped design the reality in which I lived, and I am grateful for the experiences. I am not proud of these stories, nor am I am ashamed of them, they are simply what happened.

<u>Belief 1:</u> The first people of course that we blame for everything is our parents. I blamed mine for me dropping out of high school when I was 16. For years, it was my mother's fault because she had forced me to go and live with another family miles from anything or anyone else, all because her boyfriend didn't like me. Then, later, that anger and blame turned toward my father, it was really his fault because he had allowed me to go and live with her.

<u>Reality check:</u> *I wanted to drop out of high school because it bored me. I was more interested in going out and looking for random sex partners. I would skip school to go cruising in the local parks or malls and then write notes to cover my absence. I wanted to be on my own. As far as*

being shipped down to my mother's it was my father who had allowed me to go but only as a last resort. I was not making life on him or the family easy. I was a rebel, and I wanted to live with my mother because I knew that there would be no rules. I wanted my ears and nose pierced, and I wanted to draw, paint, cut, tear, and bleach my clothing. I wanted to have a mohawk and color my hair blue and yellow. I wanted to wear white makeup with black lipstick, nail polish and rouge. I wanted to express myself in ways that my father would not allow, so I forced his hand.

Belief 2: My inability to get a good job and get ahead in life was the Navy's fault because they would not pay for my college education as promised.

Reality check: *I got myself thrown out because I was codependent. I fell in love for the first time, and when I was supposed to leave port for a 6 month deployment, I faked a suicide attempt. The night before we left, I took about 15 niacin pills in order to flush my face and laid down on the deck near my rack until someone found me. I let them pump my stomach and admit me into a psyche ward. It was there that I admitted that I was gay. Three months later, I was out of the Navy, without a boyfriend and zero idea what to do. I remember thinking to myself, well what do gay people do? Hair. So I signed up for beauty for school.*

Belief 3: I would have had a career in the beauty industry if my garage apartment hadn't burned down and my dad would have let me live with him so I could finish school.

Reality check: *I had multiple opportunities to buckle down and finish the last hundred hours of my schooling. I was just too lazy to do it. I had some crazy notion, or rather excuse, that the market was already saturated with gay hairstylists, and there would be too much competition to ever really make it big. So why bother.*

Belief 4: I am responsible for everything that goes wrong, I am the bad guy and can't do anything right. I would quit jobs in the fear that I was going to get fired for standing up for myself or for taking a sick day. I wouldn't take a sick day in fear of not having a job when I got back. After all, If I wasn't there, then they would realize I wasn't needed. I knew they would let me go when I got back, so, screw it, since that's how they felt, I would quit first.

Reality check: *I have plowed through over 100 jobs that way. I averaged 5 jobs a year for a long time. One year, I had 13 different jobs. I would get bored easily, and, more often than not, the boss always seemed less capable of running things than me, so I'd walk out. It is bizarre that this core belief could coexist with the other belief that I was not responsible for anything. This is called the martyr complex, and it is a twin sister to what I call* premeditated victimhood *in that I was able to use the situation to gain the power of the martyr energy in order to manipulate others.*

I lived, breathed, and owned these beliefs for so long, my perspective of the world was contorted. I reveled in my agony, pulling scabs from old wounds so that they reopened and couldn't heal. I suffered like this for years, always able to find the connection between why I wasn't able to catch a break or get ahead of the game and how it was never my fault. I was the victim. Or so I thought.

Then it happened. The universe provided me with the opportunity to find the serenity and happiness that seemed to be constantly eluding me through one of the most traumatic experiences of my life. I was bashed in the place I called home by people I knew. I will share the story but not the details, as they are not important.

The Art Of Self Destruction

I was sleeping in my rented garage room when the door was broken down, and three men entered with baseball bats and began to beat me up. I did my best attempt to protect myself by balling up in my sheets. When the beating was done, I sat in the darkness crying to myself and hating God for every bad thing that had ever happened in my life and wishing that I could just have some amount of peace and happiness. I didn't understand how that could be too much to ask.

The night turned to day, so I took my shower and examined my bruised body in the mirror. As I looked at my damaged body, I thought it was a good thing that I had already found a place to live, considering I was renting my room from the on again off again girlfriend and baby mama of the man who had just lead the assault.

I didn't go to work that day. Instead, I went to see the woman I had recently agreed to rent a room from. I showed up at her house with a bruised body and my story of why I needed to move in before I had all the required money. I thought for sure that there would be no way this woman would tell me that I couldn't move in right away. She seemed really nice, and I was sure to get my way. That is not what happened. Instead, that day was the first day I can remember that someone compassionately listened to me in such a way that I felt heard and then looked me in my eyes and said, "No. I told you that you could move in when you had all the money and not before. I am sorry that happened to you, but you will have to find a way to deal with your situation."

What the heck? I couldn't believe it. She could see the bruises on my arms, I had made sure to point them out, and she knew I had a job. I didn't understand at all and left her house hurt but not angry. I had been forced into a position of having to figure it out. And I did. I went to the parents of my best friend and asked them for the money. I knew that if I told them what had happened, they would feel sorry for me and help me out. I got the money, moved in that same day, and unwittingly began a journey of self-discovery and freedom from manipulating others and being controlled by circumstance.

Once I had unpacked the few things I owned, my new landlord asked me why I hadn't called the police and reported being bashed. I told her that it wasn't worth it because I worked with his girlfriend and I didn't want to cause problems at my job. I also knew that the police in the area would not be sympathetic, and I didn't want to deal with any kind of retaliation without protection. I just wanted to move on. A week or so went by, and I was approached at work by the old landlord who wanted a month's rent because I did not give her the proper 30 day move out notice. I laughed at her and told her to sue me for it. That night, I received a phone call from the lead attacker, and he told me that if I did not pay the money, he would go to the barn where I boarded my horse and break her legs. I immediately called the police and reported the whole incident and the subsequent threat toward my horse. The police went to talk with my attacker about the situation, and later that night, the police returned to my new residence and wanted to talk to me and find out what all I knew about him. Because of past experiences, I began to get concerned that he had somehow turned the tables and made me the bad guy. But then the Sheriff informed me that it took 6 police officers to take him into custody, and they found $10k cash on him and a bunch of drugs in his car as well as several guns. They wanted to make sure I felt safe. It was scary to realize how dangerous he really was. I felt in that moment that I was lucky to be alive.

Over the next couple of months as the case worked its way through the court system, I started feeling more and more like a victim and feeling angry about being a victim. I was in pain, and it was being expressed in the only way I knew how to express it, through anger, blaming, and complaining. At the time, Carin had 25 years in AA and 17 years in CODA, or Co-dependents Anonymous, and had been working as a counselor for 25 or more years. When I asked for help, she gave it. She helped me forgive him. It was that moment my life began to change. She helped me to see that I was at the core of my problems, that I was creating the emotional pain I suffered from, and that I was my own jailor.

That bashing happened in 2003, and I have spent the last 17 years finding my way out of that dark and dreary jungle. Sometimes taking one step forward and two back, but in the process, I have found my joy, and I live in it, every day. I indulge in my freedom from anger, blaming, and complaining. I am no longer looking to catch a break. I create my own opportunities, and I have learned that having control over anything other than my own words and actions is an illusion. I have learned that in order to have control over my emotional outbursts and anger, I had to forgive the people who had hurt me, and then forgive myself. I have learned that there is great power in surrender and vulnerability. Most importantly, I ACCEPTED that my anger and self-destructive way of relating with others was a disease called codependency and became willing to do whatever was necessary to end the chokehold it had on my life. I have learned how to use this thing we call "the mind" properly as the tool it is instead of letting the tool use me.

I have escaped, and you will too.

So, here is the deal. I can tell you without a doubt that if you are willing to get the heck out of your own way and apply at least three of these techniques for as little as 90 days, you will get better, and you will experience the following benefits.

- You will be more enjoyable to be around.

- Your friends and family will notice a change for the better and ask you about it.

- You will have better work and personal relationships.

- You will be happier.

  - You will experience a renewed sense of hope and optimism.

Over the next several chapters, we will explore new opportunities for growth. I will offer you easy to understand and real life examples of how anger and codependency feed on each other and how whining, blaming, and complaining only deepen the pit of misery and make it more difficult to escape. You will learn a variety of tools and how to apply them to your life so that you can have the life you want. You will come to understand your mind in a new way and, in so doing, begin to use it in new and creative ways.

This is a journey only a hero would embark on. It is one filled with discovery, pain, heartache, and, ultimately, joy. Learn from it and remember to only take what you like and what works for you and leave the rest.

The great thing is that when you begin applying what you learn in this book, you will begin to recognize, with a grateful heart, all the opportunities that have been present on your path the entire time. Who knows, you may even decide it is time to follow through with one of those old ideas you locked away so long ago.

A new path to travel.

On this path, let the heart be your guide.
— Rumi

I know you have probably read multiple self-help books, all with outstandingly empty results. Why have you failed all those other times, and why will you experience success this time? Because I am going to teach you how to succeed. I am not just going to tell you what I did to gain my freedom, I am going to give you real world examples of how to apply these tools to your life.

Why Me

I am not a doctor or LMHC, and I do not wish to be. I am a regular guy who found freedom from a life of shooting myself in the foot and self-inflicted suffering. I clawed my way out of a pit of despair and rage so intense that I would break my own things and jump into one unhealthy relationship after another. I cannot offer scholarly advice nor a diagnosis for the way you behave, but I can share with you what I have learned. However, I can only share it in the way I learned it—compassionately brutal.

The nice thing is, because I've already done the research and trial and error, and because I don't believe that you need to experience the brutality of your past any longer, I am going to give you all the compassionate part without much of the brutality. The only brutality you will experience here is in facing the truth. And, as you know, that can be painful. But the changes you will be making here will be worth the little bit of discomfort you may face in uncovering who you really are underneath it all. You will find that you are more powerful, more compassionate, and more capable of deep expressions of love and of being loved than you ever believed.

In the last 17 years, I have changed my life completely. I bulldozed over what was there and started anew. I went from seeking jobs where survival and money was the driving factor to being self-employed for the last 14 years and living better than I ever dreamed. I have read hundreds of books about love addiction, codependency, anger, rage, meditation, spirituality, qigong, Ayurveda, the art of healing, and on and on, all in search for that one missing piece.

I started my campaign for freedom by reading eastern spiritual books, then I started attending a local CoDA meeting. Once I had that initial taste of freedom, I was hooked. I began to find ways to amplify the good feelings of success.

I quickly became a Certified Healing Touch Practitioner and then a Massage Therapist, and during my 14 years working in massage, I studied Aroma therapy, Shiatsu, Kinesiology, Ortho-Bionomy, and Reflexology. I became a Reiki Master, Certified Conscious Living Coach, Ayurvedic Mind Coach, Certified QiGong Instructor, Certified Breath Empowerment Coach, as well as having sponsored and worked the 12 Steps with multiple people in CoDA . I have had my numbers read and charted by numerologists, I know my "Human Design," I am familiar and am very good at reading Medicine Cards, and my intuitive abilities have grown exponentially. I have studied and taught Non-Violent Communication skills and have applied the principles learned in the program of CoDA to my life.

There are some teachers I lean toward, like Carolyn Myss, Eckhardt Tole, and the mystics like Rumi, Jesus, and the Buddha. I have been on multi-day silent retreats and lead prayer circles with hundreds of energy and qigong practitioners all holding hands, breathing and moving in unison while holding the single thoughtform of love in their hearts and minds. I have gone to the depths of "woo woo" and returned with amazing skills and wisdom. I have taken what works for me and let the stuff that didn't feel right for me go.

I share basic information that I've learned freely with the clients I work with and will do the same here for you because you may find a better way to make life work for you, but I do not believe it to be my responsibility to drag you down one path over another, so you will get a general introduction to a verity of tools, but it is up to you to follow or further explore the rabbit hole.

What does this mean for you? It means that, yes, I do have some of the answers you want. I do know what works because I haven't just read about it or heard a lecture about it. I have lived it, and, now, you get my 17 years of experience in an easy to understand guide on how you can have the life you want.

Why You

The challenge is accepting that the missing piece is not really missing at all, it's just covered up with the piles and piles of crap that you've been tossing on it over the years. Every time you raged, lied to yourself or to someone else, you covered up who you really are. When you took what wasn't yours, when you manipulated other people, and every time you sold yourself short, you pilled more crap onto your eternal light, hiding it from you and the rest of the world. Every time you bent to the will of your fear or anger, you covered up your happiness and limited your ability to be successful. Not anymore! I am giving you a shovel, and it's time to starting digging.

I am going to show you some tools that will help you uncover and reclaim your eternal light. You will be uncovering the identity you were born into this world with and will take with you to the next lifetime. This is a process of waking up and taking responsibility for what you create as your reality. It is a process of learning how to navigate your world with a new set of senses. It is learning how to look at your mind as a tool that interrupts data provided to it from the senses instead of as your identity.

The changes you seek to make in the way you move through the world can at times feel as easy as breathing, and at other times, you will feel as if it is just too much or that you have jumped all the way back to the starting line. That's okay! You did not get where you are overnight, so do not expect to undo it overnight. You will get better and more aware with every misstep you take.

5 Truths About You

*All truth passes through three stages. First, it is
ridiculed. Second, it is violently opposed.
Third, it is accepted as being self-evident.*
– Arthur Schopenhauer

I believe in human truths and Universal truths. These concepts are only slightly related to objective or subjective truth in that only one can be proven by man. Human truths are scientific in nature, and, like objective truth, contain within them facts that can be upheld under scrutiny. Whereas Universal truths are those beliefs that can neither be proven nor disproven, except by the collective consciousness or the primordial om.

I believe the following 5 to be Universal Truths about all human beings.

25

1.   *You Are Not Broken*

You have behaved as if you are broken, other people have told you are broken or not good enough, and at times, you have believed it, and, more likely than not, you have begun to own that story. And if you're like most other people who suffer from anger issues, codependency, addiction, or past trauma, as hard as you try to be positive and do the right thing, the world and you regularly add to the negative plot line of your story with one self-sabotaging move after another. Only a broken person would do that, right?

Wrong.

Let me give you an example: I have watched several seasons of *Survivor* and on a couple of them, the winners of a contest will have some chickens given to them as a reward. The show will usually give the winners 3 chickens, which consist of two hens and a rooster. When the contestants get back to camp, they will, more often than not, end up killing and eating a hen or even both hens before the rooster. Now, anyone who grew up having to care for chickens on the farm is watching them kill the hens first and thinking, "What are these people doing?" You start to wonder how intelligent they could possibly be after doing something so blatantly stupid. I mean, really, how damaged do you have to be to kill a hen before a rooster?   Are they broken? No, they are not broken or stupid or damaged.   They just haven't been taught about chickens, just like you haven't been exposed to the information you need to make the best choices for you.

On this journey, you, like many of the clients in my office, will begin to see how you have been convinced by others and that negative voice in your head that there was or is something wrong with you, but the truth is—at your center, you are pure perfection. I want you to consider that in all respective faiths of the world, there is one God who created all that there is. There is a collectively held belief that God is perfect. Now, if you believe in God or a higher power, and you believe that God is perfect and that God created you, then you must also begin to accept the truth that you were also created perfect just like you are.

You are not broken—you just haven't been shown how to use the tools you have.

2.   *2. You are the Co-creator of All of Your Experiences*

You are here to experience that which you have created as part of "source," "the primordial om," or your "eternal self." You are the worker of the loom of life, weaving into the fabric of your existence all the experiences you've had or ever will have. All the good, the bad, the pretty, the ugly, the joy, the pain, all of it is of your creation. It is true that you cannot have light without dark, nor can you experience the true joy of love without experiencing the dark depths of hate, but you are ultimately co-creating all of it. Sometimes you are creating consciously, but because you have not been shown how to properly direct your energy, you are mostly co-creating on an unconscious level, which leads to negative consequences, whining, blaming, and complaining.

As an active co-creator you must learn to observe with compassion rather than judgement. No experience is right or wrong until you put your lens of judgement upon it, and let me assure you, your lens of judgement is not neutral, nor is it kind. It is splattered with all the negative experiences, belief patterns, learned social biases, pressure from collective consciousness, your environment, and the persuasion of those you surround yourself with.

When you learn to stop judging the experience as right or wrong and instead simply allow it to unfold, you begin to see the truth. Everything is happening exactly like it is supposed to happen. How do I know that to be true? If it has already happened, then it cannot have happened a different way because it is already in the past. Goofy logic? No, because the reality is, you can only assert change to that which has not yet taken place.

It is your responsibility to learn how to ride the wave of unfolding experiences, learning to remain in a state of continual recalibration like a surfer who is able to read the changes in the water supporting his board and shifts his weight accordingly. He does not judge what is happening as good or bad, he simply responds in the most appropriate way to get the best ride out of each wave and make it back to the beach safely. Later on, he may evaluate the ride, but in the moment, he provides no resistance to the wave.

Through choosing to implement three or more of the tools I am sharing with you here for at least 90 days, you will begin to create more enjoyable experiences in your everyday life as you learn to ride the wave rather than survive the wave.

3.   *3. You Have the Power to Forgive*

You do have the power to forgive, and in order for you to get what you want from your life, you will need to learn how to use the power of forgiveness. You will need to learn how forgive the people in your past who have harmed you, whether it be physically, mentally, emotionally or spiritually, and you will need to learn a kind of automatic forgiveness for all of those people who will inevitably cause you anguish, frustration, or pain in the future. This is how you become free from other peoples' actions.

It is also imperative that you learn how to forgive yourself, but here is another truth; you cannot forgive yourself until you have truly learned to forgive others. Why do you need to forgive yourself for what someone else did? Because, even if you are the victim of something as extreme as an unprovoked act of violence or as common as an internet scam, your mind will find a way to put some of the blame on you. That voice in your head will make you believe you were somehow at fault for being beat up when that gang who jumped you came out of nowhere, after all, you were the idiot who rented a room from a women who had a violent boyfriend. Or if you have been the victim of a scam, you will always be able to go back and see where you made your mistake. You cannot just blow the stuff off as a lesson, not until you have forgiven that part of you who feels guilt, shame, or blame around any issue.

If there is someone in your life who you believe you have forgiven but you're not sure, here is how you tell. Think of that person and whatever it was that they did, and if you feel anything but acceptance, then you have not fully forgiven them. Keep reading, you will get there, and if you do not find the path for forgiveness, you will at least live with acceptance.

29

Be brave and be prepared to receive the greatest gift you have ever given yourself.

4.   *4. You Are Always Teaching*

This truth is the most important truth if you are a parent, especially the parent of a small child, because you are always teaching them how to show love, be loved, be a mother, father, wife, husband, man, women, brother, or sister, so you have a huge responsibility. You are teaching your children how a wife treats a husband and how a father treats a daughter, and it goes well beyond the immediate family. You are teaching your boss, your friends, coworkers, and everyone else you interact with how to treat you. So check yourself, do you allow your boss or supervisor to act inappropriately but do nothing about it and then go home and complain to your significant other about what a horrible person your boss is all they while telling your kids not to talk about others behind their back? Does a loved one or significant other verbally or physically abuse you but you do nothing about it, yet expect your friend or child to stand up to their bullies?

Check yourself here because you and you alone are responsible for teaching others how to treat you, and you are teaching others what is and is not acceptable behavior in your presence. If you idly stand by and watch someone being victimized, you are teaching others that you are okay with the injustice that you and they are witnessing.

If you have watched an episode of the ABC News program *What Would You Do?* you'll know what I am talking about because average people are put into situations where they can choose to either stand by and watch a negative bias play out or take a stand and intervene. It reminds me of the saying attributed to Edmund Burke, "The only thing necessary for the triumph of evil is for good men/people to do nothing."

What are you teaching the world?

5.   *5. You Have Freewill and the Right to Choose*

This is a powerful statement and can mean all sorts of things to you on many different levels, or it could be the one thing that singularly defines your personal truth going forward. To have freewill means to have choice.   Each day, with every decision you make and every thoughtform you follow through to its end result, you are making choices. Or, at least that is how it is for a balanced person who knows how to handle challenges as they come up. However, when you carry around resentment, anger, or jealousy and see things through tainted glasses, you lose your power of choice, and you go through life unconsciously reacting to stimuli instead of considering the information and responding with the next appropriate action or inaction.

I want you to image your past hurts or traumas as the pinball in a pinball machine. Watch as you or someone else launches the ball from the ball shooter and it heads up the lane and onto the playfield. Once on the playfield, watch as the ball frantically bounces from one bumper and slams into another, gaining momentum as it randomly contacts the drop targets and spinners. Notice that all of this is happening with no help from you. After the ball is launched, you have no choice as to how the ball is going to move about the playfield, but you do have the choice to keep the ball in play with the flippers or allow it to enter the drain. Are you keeping balls in play unnecessarily?

Ruts

Here is another truth about choice and freewill. Suffering is a choice. If you are suffering from emotional, spiritual, or philosophical pain, and even some forms of physical pain, it is a choice. That's right, and I will say it again, suffering is a choice. You and you alone decide or choose to carry the pain from the past into the present moment and paint your world with that ugliness. No one is holding a gun to your head and telling you to drag what happened to that child you once were into the here and now but you and your need for an excuse.

Choose. Do you want to allow that old stuff to control the rest of your life, or do you want to take back control of your life from the people you say stole it but in reality the people to whom you gave it to and continue to give it to?

How many times have you been driving down the interstate and you decide to pass the vehicle ahead that is slowing down progress, and, being the awesome driver you are, you signal your intent to pass and start to turn the steering wheel only to find that the road is so well traveled that the tires are resisting your instructions and attempting to keep you in your current lane of travel, you can actually feel the pull on the steering wheel. What do you do? Do you give up and just stay behind the person going slower than you want to travel, or do you decide to force the issue and turn the vehicle out of the grooved pavement of that lane and get past the vehicle that is slowing progress?

Right here, right now, I want you to take back some power and decide, are you going to choose to be a victim of past circumstances and hang out in the slow lane, or will you choose something different and change your lane of travel?

Choose now.

Energy

You are pure vibrational energy. Quantum studies have proven that everything we are and experience is at its core—energy. Einstein had a lot to say about energy, and these two things I find most interesting and useful when it comes to understanding how we hold onto emotions and how we release emotions. He said that energy can become matter, and matter can become energy, and that energy can neither be created nor destroyed, it can only be changed from one form to another.

Understanding this and learning to apply it on an emotional level, you will begin to free yourself from the wrongs of the past, even those past wrongs and traumas that are being stored below your conscious level and living in your nervous system as emotional resonance.

What is emotional resonance? Well, let me first explain resonance. Musicians will be familiar with the term but for all you others, if you were to take two guitars and put them in the same room but in opposite corners and pluck the G string on only one of them, the G string on the other guitar will begin to sympathetically vibrate, this is resonance. When applied to your emotions, resonance works like this; unresolved emotions are held or are resonating in the nervous system just waiting for an external amplifier or trigger to create a valve so that the built up negative energy can be released. So you can be in a neutral mood and someone will say something that unconsciously resonates with an old hurt and you react, or, rather, over react, to whatever was said or done with no conscious understanding of why.

We can also refer back to the pinball analogy for this one, but in this instance, the ball would be whatever is said or done by the outside party and that is launched onto the internal playfield via the nervous system, and the bumpers, spinners, and drop targets are the past hurts, traumas, etc., or the emotional resonance. You see, the person who set the ball into play had no say or choice in what the ball would come into contact with once it was launched, and only you can choose to allow the ball to leave the play area either by the drain, letting it go, or by housing only passive bumpers or bumpers that carry no charge.

By applying the techniques in this book, you will stop reacting inappropriately and snapping at people for "no reason." You will be setting yourself free on all levels, and you will be able to truly exert freewill and have a wider selection of choices.

In the next 7 chapters, we will explore various tools and processes that you can use to set off on a new path in life and get the things you want. One that is filled with more success and is more fulfilling because you will have more choices.

At this point, I want to remind you of the promise I made earlier.

If you are willing to get the heck out of your own way and apply at least three of these techniques for as little as 90 days, you will get better, and you will experience the following benefits.

- You will be more enjoyable to be around.

- Your friends and family will notice a change for the better and ask you about it.

- You will have better work and personal relationships.

- You will be happier.

- You will experience a renewed sense of hope and optimism.

Understanding Your Mind

*"You have power over your mind—not outside events.
Realize this, and you will find strength."*
— Marcus Aurelius

When you think about your mind, what are you considering? What is your mind? Is it the electrical signals that flow through the neural pathways of the brain, or is it something altogether different? Do you understand the nature of your mind? Do you believe that your mind and your brain are one and the same? Where does awareness and consciousness fit into the picture?

These are questions that most of the clients I work with have never considered and that we will now begin to explore. But please be aware that I am only going to touch the surface or fringes of these ideas, as I want you to decide for yourself how deeply down the rabbit hole you wish go.

The White Rabbit

What is the nature of your mind? This is a question that has been pondered by great yogi's, philosophers, and scientists alike, and no clear picture has yet been developed. Your mind is at work in all states of consciousness and unconsciousness and is of a quantum nature, meaning that you are only aware of it when you are observing it. In other words, your mind is not physical in nature, i.e. the brain. Rather, it has structure in the form of subtle conditions and energies that can be observed through tangible and verifiable effects, which means that you can recognize the influence it has on the outer world through your experiences, or, on a physical level, this influence is recognized as feelings due to the release of neuropeptides. Just like you can see and use your hands and your feet, your awareness recognizes and uses your mind. The mind is in constant motion and is always thinking for it cannot exist without thinking as it is made up of thought, and it is those thoughts that make up your reality. In other words, it is always considering, planning, reacting emotionally, or looking for other ways to create engagement with our sensory experiences. It is responsible for the overseeing of thought into form.

In order to learn how to see the workings of the mind, you must become the observer of the mind and step outside the activity that is taking place within it. Basically, if you are driving your car with your eyes on your cell phone, you can't pay attention to what's happening on the road around you. You must become the observer of your thoughts, emotions, and actions in order to not only understand them but to gain a deeper knowledge of yourself and how best to meet your needs and wants even as challenges appear. Just like in order to safely drive your car from one place to another, you need to know how to operate the vehicle, and you need to keep your attention on what is happening around you and continually make adjustments to your speed and your direction of travel as well adjusting to any environmental conditions that may arise like a sudden rain storm or high winds.

Consider that you do not go through the day thinking about how to use your brain to think, the mind just does it. Just like you don't think about using your throat to swallow when you drink something, your body just does it. And so, just like the muscles that make swallowing happen are not the throat, the brain is not the mind. Yet the mind uses your brain to complete its tasks or think your thoughts, and it uses it 24/7, but it is not of the brain, nor is it limited to its use. The mind does not reside in one location, it moves to where your awareness goes. It is attached to the outside world, and because of its dualistic nature, the mind by itself is not equipped to make intelligent choices. To make a fully intelligent choice, you need balance in heart and mind with consciousness and awareness.

Painting the Roses

You lose your power over the mind when you start to allow it to direct your thoughts and actions. Once you give your mind the power to run things, you no longer have control of your life, you've become the pinball bouncing chaotically off everything that happens. In order to retake control, you must learn to quiet the mind and stop experiencing life through it and start to experience it through the eyes of your observer. By doing so, you are no longer personalizing the outer world or what is happening, and when you stop doing that, you are better able to see the reality of things. Objectivity sets in and provides you with a sense of empowerment as you are more clearly able to find solutions to the challenges that you're faced with big and small.

So, if the mind is not the brain, it is not aware, it is not intelligent, and you are not the mind, what is it? Or, rather, what is its function? When you look at the function of the mind, you first notice that it is always driving us to do things. It is in constant movement, which causes conflict, and that in turn propels choice, and that creates more movement, and round and round we go until we learn to reclaim control. The basic underlying function of the mind is to be an instrument used by your awareness to understand the physical or outer world as well as the internal or emotional world—to make sense of it, or, rather, to correlate all the input into meanings that our consciousness can understand and use, aka intelligence.

Tea Party

This is where things get a little trippy, because when I talk about awareness, I am speaking about the eternal self. You see, awareness is not bound to time or space, it has no form or function, and it has no regard for good, bad, right, or wrong, and awareness does not bring about consciousness, nor does consciousness bring about awareness. Like the mind and the brain, the two are tied to each other but not of each other. Consciousness uses awareness like the mind uses the brain. Let me explain it this way; a comatose person upon waking up will often say that they were aware of everything that was going on around them, though never showing any sings of consciousness, and a conscious person can remain in a debilitative state of unawareness for years, seemingly trapped in an internal world. Consciousness without awareness is as useless as awareness without consciousness, as there is no decreeable level of intelligence in either one alone. Which means that until consciousness and awareness are teamed up, you lack true intelligence.

What does all that mean? It means that you must understand and master how your mind is using the information gathered by your senses, and in so doing, you gain control of your mind, and you are able to make conscious choices rather than simply react. It means that when your heart and your mind are congruent in the choices you make, you are using all of your intelligence.

You must learn to manage your mind in order to get what you want. If you allow your mind to constantly focus on negative thoughts, then you are doomed to live in a negative world with very few joyful experiences, the world of resistance. The goal here is to actually get to the point where you no longer have to manage negative thoughts because they are no longer what the mind gives energy or power too. Not saying that bad stuff won't happen, but once resolved, it won't be swimming around in your head hours, days, weeks, or years later.

Off with Her Head

One of your minds favorite ways to trick you is with a game of connect the dots even when there are no dots. This game is called cognitive fusion. Cognitive fusion is the process of attaching a thought or a feeling to an experience, or anchoring feelings and thoughts to an experience. For example, your friends have set you up on a blind date, and you are really hitting it off and magic is in the air, then you find out that your date works at the club where both of your exes cheated on you, and your mind jumps right to the conclusion that this person is a cheater and barriers are thrown up.

Through this process, your mind creates patterns and judgments that define your way of thinking and behaving or frameworks. It is a process in which you become trapped in a neverending loop of negative thinking, and you stop relating to what is taking place right in front of you. Basically, you stop being associated with the information being processed right now by the 5 senses and become enmeshed or trapped in a loop of ever-deepening disillusionment and suffering because you're fixated on some erroneous thought or belief. And when you begin to believe this negative self-talk, you activate a string of negative self-fulfilling prophecies which only strengthens the original limiting and damaging thoughts.

A framework can be as simple as believing that every day is going to be a bad day in traffic, or thoughts like, "Why do all the idiots have to be out on the road when I am?" These thoughts are negative frameworks, and they set you up for failure and anger. More importantly, you are sure to get what you want.

So, how do you know you're in a state of fusion or running an old program? As soon as your thought feels, or your mind makes it appear:

- As if you are experiencing something in the present even though it has not happened, or it happened long ago. (future tripping - regretting)

- It is the absolute truth (everyone else is wrong).

How does having an awareness of this help? By understanding how you create what I call a self-induced crisis, you have the ability to recognize the activating experience or the trigger. Once you are aware that you are about to or that you have fallen into that trap or old way of thinking, you can consciously break or interrupt the pattern and return to reality here in the present moment.

One of the most effective ways of doing that is with cognitive diffusion. Cognitive diffusion is the conscious act of observing your thoughts for what they really are, just thoughts.

When you are able to transition into a state of diffusion, your mind recognizes that the thoughts are:

- Thoughts, not something that needs to be acted on or even considered for more than what they are, just thoughts.

- are possibly inaccurate.

When you are able to observe your thoughts as simply thoughts, without judgment or attachment, and subject them to an internal inquiry, you are able to experience life with less suffering and more love, peace, and serenity.

Innocent Tart Thief

You will need to start to question those thoughts that take your energy in a negative direction so that you can end the cycle. When you notice a thought that is negative, ask yourself, "Why is this thought currently receiving my attention?" Is it generated by fear? If so, what do I think I am at risk of losing?

Is this thought true, or has it been tainted by an old, out of date framework? Meaning; is the thought based in reality, or are you tricking yourself again by hiding from responsibility or looking for a way to blame someone else?

Once you free yourself from the internal conflict and the trap of fusion, you can focus on what your higher intentions are. You become free, and your internal success machine, that is your unconscious mind, starts to work in alignment with your conscious desires, and instead of a day filled with one disappointment after another, you have a life filled with abundance, joy, and love.

Here are two exercises to help you learn about the nature of your mind. In the next chapter, you will learn how to recognize habitual patterns of thinking or behavior, aka your regular lane of travel, and become actively involved in creating new thought patterns and new behaviors that will actually help you along your path.

- Choose some sort of object, like an animal or plant, and notice that as you focus on it, your attention bounces all over the place like that pinball from earlier, and every time it comes in contact with a bumper, an idea or belief is formed about the object, creating a deeper sense of the object. Now, attempt to focus your attention on only one aspect of the object, and notice how your attention cannot be held there long before it shoots off to notice something else.

- Next, observe what effects your emotions have on how you use your mind or how it functions. Become familiar with how fear, anger, and joy can increase and diminish the power of your thoughts. Watch your thoughts and notice how they appear to follow one after another in rapid succession like thunder and lighting, and at times with no seeming continuity.

Your Energetic System

When you are working well with your energy, you are also
making the best expression of your personal power...
By reading your own energy, by becoming aware of the lens
through which you see your world, you can change your
mind and change your life.
— Caroline Myss

You have been taught about your nervous system, your circulatory system, and all the rest of your bodily systems in your high school biology or health class, but you won't find a class on the human energy system anywhere on the schedule. Granted, some of you may be familiar with the human energy system, and that is awesome because you are going to learn how to start to put it work for you while others may not have a clue about what it is, and that is perfect too because you're right where you need to be in order to learn how to harness this amazing power.

Energy

Like your mind the human energy system interacts with but is not a part of the human body, and, like the quantum nature of the mind, your energetic system has a tangible and variable effect through your experiences. When the main system, which is made up of three subsystems, is balanced, and all three aspects are working as one, you experience what is called being in a state of flow.

When I talk about the human energy system, I am referring to the whole of it, but in order to understand the whole of it, you need a clearer picture of the smaller components that are related to the aspect of the mind, body, and spirit.

The mind aspect of the energy system is made up of archetypal energy patterns, and it is the aspect that is most useful in understanding your behavior patterns and beginning to change them, so I will discuss this last.

The body aspect is made up the mappable energy system of the physical body like accu-points.

And then there is the spiritual aspect or the ethereal nature of our energetic system, which is comprised of the well know chakra system, which I will cover only lightly.

Most ancient eastern philosophies include some form of teaching related to the energy pathways in the human body. In Ayurveda, they are referred to as marma points, in acupuncture, they are called meridians, and in Reiki, they are referred to as tandens. Working with these specific points result in the movement and balancing of energy or qi or prana in and around the body. So, if you work with a Reiki master, healing touch practitioner, acupuncturist, reflexologist, or any energy practitioner, they are all working with and balancing the flow of energy in and between the chakras which are the major power centers within this energetic system. This balancing is being achieved, or at least amplified, through these physical or bodily pathways and channels. They can be likened to an energetic vortex for the human body similar to the energy vortexes found in Arizona and around the planet.

The chakra system is well documented, and the topic is covered in many a book, so I will only touch on some of the more important pieces because this is the part of the energy system that creates the most havoc on your physical body. Your energetic system is speaking to you on a regular basis through the way you feel physically. It is reflected in the illness you suffer from, and it is the basis for the power behind the concept of the biology of belief. The biology of belief is the hypothesis that DNA is controlled by signals from outside the cell, including the energetic messages emanating from our positive and negative thoughts.

Here is a chart demonstrating the mental, emotional, and physical relationship inherent to each one.

Chakra	Mental / Emotional Relationship	Physical Relationship
1	Ability to stand up for yourself, feeling at home, worry	Chronic low back pain, depression, immune system dysfunction
2	Blame, guilt, money, sex, power, control, creativity	Chronic low back pain, pelvic floor pain, urinary issues, sexual issues
3	Trust, decision making, Self-esteem, self-respect, Fear	Easting disorders, abdominal issues, arthritis, liver issues, adrenal issues
4	Love, hate, resentment, grief, anger, loneliness, selfishness	All respiratory and circulatory system issues, breast cancer
5	Addiction, decision making, judgement, faith	Scoliosis, thyroid, nose, mouth, jaw and throat issues
6	Truth, Inadequacy, emotional intelligence, self-evaluation	Learning disabilities, spinal issues, seizures, stroke
7	Values, ethics, courage, selflessness, faith	Extreme sensitivities to environmental factors, philosophical depression

When you slow down and begin to reflect on the issues that are plaguing your life and what kind of energetic signature those issues carry, you will be able to more easily identify the need, want, or desire that needs to be addressed. If you want to work with an energy practitioner, I suggest you follow the same guidelines I present in the It's *Okay to Ask For Help* chapter.

What are archetypes and why is it so important to understand them? Archetypes have been discussed since the time of Plato. Plato's *ideas,* or the so-called Platonic *eidos,* were pure mental forms that were imprinted in the soul before it was born into the world. Then came Carl Jung, in who's psychological framework, archetypes are innate, universal prototypes for ideas and may be used to interpret observations, and his ideas later became a model for others like Carolyn Myss to build upon, giving us the easily understandable model that is most commonly used today.

As discussed, your energetic system is helping to create your physical experiences with your negative or positive thoughts, but what is in charge of the negative or positive charge associated with the thought? It is the influence on the mind by the archetype that is currently sitting in the driver's seat or who has control of the executive function of the brain. It is ultimately your mind, and like you learned earlier, your mind has been programmed to react one way or another given the situation, and like you found out earlier, you must learn to manage your thoughts in order to respond instead of react so that you get what you want and in order to see the world as it is.

Once you understand the energy behind your motivations you will have access to greater options. As you are introduced to these energetic patterns, you will be amazed at how they impact your life and the importance of learning how to work with them in order to get the best out of yourself and those around you. Understanding how to work with your archetypes gives you power to create change in areas of your life where you have given up hope to change. You will begin to work with the power inherent in each archetype I will discuss here, giving you a start to a new kind of understanding of who you are and what your higher purpose is.

Like awareness uses your mind, archetypes use your awareness. They perceive through it, and it is their job to direct you toward your greatest possibilities. I am only going to discuss the four survival archetypes that everyone has in common. These include The Child, The Prostitute, The Victim, and The Saboteur. The model developed by Carolyn Myss in Scared Contracts discusses a total of twelve archetypes, one for each of the 12 astrological houses, and they rule the power of that house, but that aspect is not important for learning how to manage the basic four and to get you started.

The four survival archetypes can be considered the intimate companions of your intuition—listen to them and you will not go wrong. They influence how you respond to authority, your ability to make choices, and how you use your material power. You should know that all archetypes are essentially neutral by design and manifest in both light and shadow attributes. It is also important to understand that you experience each of your archetypes through the shadow side of the energy before experience the light side.

There are more than 70 in total, but as I said, you embody a total of 12, and when you understand the nature of the archetypes, it is easy to call upon those energies and allow them to take control of the executive functions, or a set of processes that have to do with managing yourself and your resources in order to achieve a goal, aka your mind. When you allow that to happen, especially during a challenging situation, you can be more easily guided by your higher power acting through your intuition.

The influence that these energies have over your life is significant and can be easily recognized when you get to know their patterns. For example: The Rebel and Destroyer archetypes make up part of my 12, and when reviewing my life from the 7th grade until my early 30's, it is easy to see the shadow side of these living out loud. The rebel was the first to show itself, and boy oh boy did my dad and mom have fun with that, especially my father, who I would defy at every opportunity. The energy of the rebel will defy authority just to defy authority, or because what is being asked is difficult or uncomfortable. On the light side, this is the energy that defies the collective idea of religion or spirituality and can lead you in a different direction and your own understating of a higher power. It is the energy that pushes change forward. All of these identifiable patterns, both the shadow and the light, can be seen in my life from childhood into present day. As I child, I rebelled against my parents, then as a teen, I rebelled against social norms and standards by having a multicolored mohawk, then moved into my late teens and twenties when I was part of ActUP and any other movement that pushed the gay agenda for equal rights forward, and now I am still doing what I can to fight social injustice. The energy of the Rebel can be seen in most people to a degree, and so it is good to be aware of it and which side of the power you are plugged into.

The Destroyer archetype is very different from the Rebel, especially the manifestation of the shadow side. The general symbolic understanding of the destroyer can be seen in the Hindu goddess Kali and the concept that in order to rebuild we must first destroy, hence the title of this book. I used the shadow aspect of this extremely powerful archetype like a knight wields a sword, and I could easily eviscerate any dream or positive idea that I had or that someone else had. And if I felt someone getting in my way, I would use this energy to destroy thier confidence and any sense of self-worth they had. That is the shadow side of the Destroyer, and it is a terribly powerful weapon. However, when I woke up and started to live consciously, I found out how to turn that weapon into a powerful force for good and have since worked with hundreds of clients who I have helped destroy their own limiting beliefs and self-destructive patterns so that they could build the lives they wanted on top of those ashes. This book was created because the experiences I had living in the shadow side of the Destroyer.

This is why it is so important for you to understand that ALL of your experiences are worthwhile, because the bad ones teach you what you need to do differently, and the good ones show you that what you are doing is working.

The 4 survival archetypes are:

The Child - The child archetype includes the orphan, wounded, eternal, magical, divine, and nature child. Each of these have their own energetic signatures, but the inherent lesson and power in all is dependency and responsibility. Do you find it difficult to take care of yourself or do you depend heavily on others to get your needs met? Food, housing, etc.? These are the energetic signatures of the shadow side of the child, but when brought into the light, the child becomes your guardian of innocence, it helps you to heal and to stop negative self-talk and self-directed emotional abuse.

Signs that you are playing in the shadows are obvious with this archetype as the people around you will usually tell you stop acting like a baby, and you definitely know when you're treating yourself badly or throwing a temper tantrum because you're not getting your way.

When you find that this energy has taken over your mindset, you need to stop, take a step back, and ask your inner child, "What do you need in order to feel safe and loved? Once you have identified the need, ask yourself what about the situation needs to be different in order for you to be okay? Then ask what do I reasonably have the power to change? What kind of creative solution can your inner child come up with? Unrestricted from the rules and limitations of the adult world, your child archetype is a creative powerhouse of solutions.

The Prostitute - The first thing you need to know here is that I am not taking about the literal prostitute who works on the dingy streets of every hometown USA, but the underlying energetic signature of the prostitute archetype lies in financial and physical survival. When your survival is threatened, this energy pattern enters its full potential, but it is active in your life on a subtle level every day. The Prostitute archetype is your guardian of faith, it presents issues that ask how much you are willing to sell of yourself, your morals, integrity, intellect, your word, body, or soul for the sake of survival. If you have no faith, you will one day come across a price that you won't turn away.

Signs that you are experiencing the shadow side of the prostitute archetype include keeping a job where you are mistreated or unappreciated because you need to pay the rent, or you could be using your seductive powers to control someone else, or you could be in a bad relationship but stay for financial reasons or because you don't want to be alone.

The prostitute archetype runs the business for many self-employed service providers such as massage therapists, acupuncturists, hypnotists and such who advertise on discount sites like groupon or livingsocial. I say this because research has proven clients that come from those sites are not looking for their next lifetime provider, they are looking for the next cheapest deal. So, regardless of the quality of service provided, the customer will not schedule a follow up session, and the practitioner is left with a sense of resentment because they worked as hard for the reduced amount as they would have for the full amount without getting the return on the investment that they wanted. They sold themselves short out of fear that they can't get enough work, and this breaks down self-worth, and that is only compounded when they see their peers who charge more succeeding.

Some examples of the prostitute archetype in the media include Michael Cohen and Donna RoTunno, both of whom are high powered attorneys and will do what is asked of them regardless of the ethical aspects. As soon as you put your ethical duties aside in business and personal relationships in order to get ahead, you are playing with the shadow side of this energy pattern.

You can start to balance this energy by moving away from situations that cost you too much money, energy, dignity, or time.

The Victim - The light side of the victim archetype acts as your guardian of self-esteem, while in the shadow, it is the energy of placing blame and using the poor me syndrome, or it can even be that you are victimizing other people to get ahead. This is the archetype that helps you create safe boundaries, both containment and personal. Containment boundaries are the internal boundaries that keep you from sharing too much with the wrong people and keeps you in line with your personal power, while personal boundaries are guidelines or limits that you establish to identify reasonable, safe, and permissible ways for other people to treat you and how you respond when someone crosses those lines. Will you continue to allow other people to victimize you, or will you take back your power and stand up for yourself?

I worked with a client who introduced me to her victim archetype on our first meeting. She was late for the session, and when she showed up, she was all in a huff. She immediately began blaming the bus and the stupid walk signals for her tardiness and did so with much flare and dramatics as she tore at her coat to get it off. The fight with the coat continued while she was frantically explaining how she is never late all the while getting more and more tightly wound until she gave up, exhausted and threw herself into a chair. She continued feeding her anxiety by advising me that this would surely ruin her session and on and on about how she never got anything right and she was so dumb that she couldn't even figure out the bus schedule, blah, blah, blah. I sat there with a kind of Mona Lisa smile on my face, knowing full well the depths of her anguish and struggle because I'd had a very close relationship with the victim archetype for many years myself, and I knew what joy she was in for once she learned how to control her thoughts. Victimization is valuable currency in the world of emotional manipulation.

When you find yourself acting like a victim or victimizing another, stop and ask yourself, "What are my options in this situation, and what can I do that WILL empower me?"

The Saboteur - You are familiar with this pattern because of the painful challenges and lesson it presents, much like the Victim and Prostitute. The Saboteur is the guardian of choice. The shadow side will sabotage your efforts to move ahead with self-doubt and second guessing your choices. This is the voice you hear in your head that says you can't do it or that you're not good enough.

When you find your mind is overrun with the negative self-talk and self-doubt of the Saboteur, shut it down by gathering your courage and questioning your fears and listen to your intuition.

The more conscious you can remain about the archetypal patterns influencing your behavior, the more likely that your choices and lessons will be positive. If your choices are made unconsciously, and you act defensively and fearfully, you may not learn and grow as you should.

The first step in regaining control and getting yourself in balance starts the moment you become aware of how you are behaving. The moment you become aware, you become responsible for each action or inaction after that, and that moment of awareness is the doorway to change and power because that is the moment that you can decide to continue to act out the same old story and behaviors, or will you stop and choose to experience something different even if you don't know what the experience may hold.

In order to gain control, you must identify the archetypal energy in play and redirect it from the shadow or negative aspect into the light or positive aspect of it.

Resistance and Surrender

Always say "yes" to the present moment.
What could be more futile, more insane,
than to create inner resistance to what already is?
What could be more insane than to oppose life itself,
which is now and always now? Surrender to what is.
Say "yes" to life — and see how life suddenly
starts working for you rather than against you.
— Eckhart Tolle

You are probably familiar with that famous Borg line, "Resistance is futile," and maybe you have seen the eastern philosophical statement, "What you resist persists" or the one by Louise Hay, "Resistance is the first step to change." Without a

58

doubt, all of these sayings fall under the category of Universal Truths.

But you are already familiar with resistance on a deeper level because you practice it on a regular basis. It is so much a part of you that you engage in it without even thinking about it. It is what you feel when what is happening is not in alignment with you want, and you know when you are resisting something because it is generally accompanied by anger or another negative emotion.

The strategy that shows to be most effective in overcoming resistance is by practicing surrender. Until you relinquish control of things that you can't control and continue to have attachment to the outcome of your endeavors, you will spend your life pushing chunks of ice up a very slippery glacier with nothing but a pair of sandals on. Get the picture? No? Okay, let me put it this way, until you are ready to surrender to the forces of natural law, the universe, God's will, the Devine unfolding, unwritten law, or whatever you want to call it, you will not win.

I know it is hard to image that surrender could be a positive thing, considering that the very definition of the word claims defeat. For example, among the Merriam-Webster Dictionary entries for the word are; to yield to the power, control, or possession of another upon compulsion or demand AND: to give (oneself) up into the power of another, especially as a prisoner.

That doesn't sound appealing, nor does it sound as if it is an appropriate strategy for getting the best out of life or yourself, but as you continue your journey, you will begin to understand the difference between the gift of surrender and giving up, defeatism, or victimhood.

The kind of surrender I am suggesting is not to a person or belief, it simply means living life on life's terms. It is a kind of spiritual surrender, a surrender to "what is." This process holds within it the ability to accept that you have no control over others or their actions and that you are not responsible for the actions of others. You are only responsible for your actions and the consequences of those actions both good and bad. It is the epitome of, "You can only do what you can do."

Here is another way to view surrender. One of the presuppositions or underlying beliefs in the world of NLP, NeuroLinguistic Programming, stipulates that the person or element with the most flexibility within a system will have the most influence over that system. This is called the Law of requisite variety and means that the person with the most options and behavioral choices will end up controlling the system, or, at the least, have the majority of influence over the system. So, basically, he who can surrender to that which is happening has a larger spectrum of choices available so they can better affect their experiences.

Effective methods for practicing surrender include:

• Stay in the present moment and remain objective. Ask yourself, "What am I resisting and why?" When I say stay in the present moment, I mean don't pile a bunch of negative things from the past onto whatever you are doing in the now. That way, you can remain objective.

- Disengage from the act of judging. That means you need to stop judging yourself and others as well as what is happening.

- Patience is a virtue. Be gentle on yourself and others, you are after all, only human.

- Take a moment. Practice some deep diaphragmatic breathing or qigong breathing or use the EFT protocol you will be learning later. (Videos and resources available for free at excelhypnosis.com.)

- Practice gratitude. I want you to do what I ask every client I work with to do, and that is to purchase a nice leather-bound notebook and write a minimum of 10 things in it every day that you are grateful for. If there are more than 10 things, great, but include no less than 10 things.

- Relax. Allow your challenges to solve themselves. This means that you need to focus your thoughts, the activity of your mind, to the things that are working well. By doing so, you are surrendering your challenges to the subconscious where all resolutions reside. Then, out of the blue, the solution will just present itself.

Forgiveness and Acceptance

Forgiveness is not an occasional act—it is a constant attitude.
– Martin Luther King, Jr.

6.

It's May 1980 and steam from the top of Mt. St. Helens is rising lazily into the clear blue skies on a warm spring afternoon, and a young 7th grade boy is out playing soccer with his friends. Suddenly, and out of nowhere, she appears, one of the sneakier bullies of the playground, and she promptly kicks him in the groin, takes the ball, and leaves him there crying, embarrassed and angry. So, the boy who is often picked on has been told by his father that he needs to start standing up for himself and decides to execute his payback later that afternoon as the entire 5th thru 8th grade classes are headed to an assembly in the gym by pulling the girl's hair. The girl tells the teacher what he has done, and he is promptly lead to the front of the assembly where he is used by three female administrators as an example of what happens to little boys who pick on little girls. He is punished, and he is humiliated and shamed in front of the entire student body by the women, and the girl is not punished for her actions.

Seeds

The affect this has on the boy's life begins immediately with him dropping out of the school choir, leaving the drama club, and within 2 months, he is kicked out of school for the first time.

As the boy became a man and entered the workforce, he was plagued with feelings of anger toward female supervisors and had no issue expressing his dislike for women who he felt disrespected men. He lost multiple jobs because he was not able to keep his anger and opinion in check with females who were in charge and unjustly used their power, especially if her actions included attempting to shame or embarrass him or another person. He sought out help from multiple sources, and the only relief he was able to find was in practicing surrender and remaining conscious of his behavior. However, not knowing what would trigger his inappropriate response, he was not always able to catch himself, and he was never able to put his finger on why he behaved the way he did.

Then he was introduced to self-hypnosis, and during his 4th day of practice, and working specifically with forgiveness as the main intent, he had a life changing experience. He did not remember the playground experience, he revivified the experience, or experienced the emotional pain and embarrassment as if it were happening to him again. He had not consciously thought about that experience for as long as he could remember and, in fact, had not remembered it'd happened until he was in trance and his subconscious mind made it possible to tap into those old records. Because he was working with forgiveness as the main intent, he followed through and forgave the females who were responsible for making him feel the shame, the embarrassment, and for not giving him the opportunity to share his side of the story.

He has never experienced an inappropriate outburst of anger toward women again over any injustice, regardless of the participants. That is the combined power of forgiveness and self-hypnosis.

You have been told over and over again how important the act of forgiveness is in achieving freedom from resentment and past trauma, and in your bid for happiness, you have gone through the motions, but you still get angry when you think about what happened, and it still effects the present moment for you and everyone you interact with. If this is the case, then you have not forgiven the offender of that past misdeed, or you have not forgiven yourself.

Forgiveness is an expression of love toward yourself and an act of unconditional love toward another. Notice the difference, when applied to yourself, it is an expression of a feeling of love, and when you apply it to another, it is an action that moves you beyond freedom and into a sense of power and joy.

The Art Of Self Destruction

You probably have not been taught a healthy way to forgive by your parents, church leaders, teachers, or any other part of society, and that is because the act of forgiveness has been reduced to a forced process of insincere actions and words. Here is an example of what children are taught about forgiveness: Joe and Adam are out playing during recess when Joe decides to take Adam's ball, and during the protest, Adam falls to the ground, scraping his knee, and Joe runs off in laughter and rejoins his friends. Adam, following the rules, approaches the recess monitor and informs him of what Joe has done. The monitor doing exactly as he is taught gathers the two boys together. He then tells Joe that what he has done is wrong and he needs to give the ball back and apologize, aka—asking for forgiveness, and Adam is told that he will accept the apology, aka —forgiving him, and then Joe and Adam are told to shake hands, and everything is set right.

Except it is not set right, because this is not asking for forgiveness, this is lip service, this is a learned and socially acceptable way to behave badly and not take responsibility for it. This also doesn't allow for forgiveness, this is a forced behavior that creates a divide, confusion, and a power imbalance.

This kind of forced forgiveness implies that the perpetrator does not have to take responsibility for his actions or inaction in any given situation. It is an inequitable contract that says if I say "I am sorry" you have to say "I forgive you," which immediately releases me of my responsibility and gives me permission to do it again. The victim is forced to tell someone who has mistreated them that they are forgiven without the benefit of understanding that forgiveness is a process that is for them, not the perpetrator, that it is a process used to free themself from the wrong doings of others. Instead, a seed of resentment is planted, and forgiveness loses its' effectiveness and meaning.

Healthy forgiveness is a process wherein you free yourself from the misdeeds of others so that you can move forward with your life leaving behind the anger, resentment, and even depression. I am not suggesting that you forgive and forget. In fact, throughout history, we have been taught that forgetting is just flat out stupid. You are not unshackling others from the ramifications of their behavior, and the people you forgive do not need to know that you have forgiven them because it's none of their business, and, like I mentioned above, some people will use that forgiveness as an excuse to trespass yet again.

All this forgiveness stuff is great for your mental, emotional, and physical health, and it seems really great in theory, but you may not be able to muster the love required to complete such a task, yet, and that's okay. You are going to get the benefit of forgiveness through a sort of pseudo forgiveness, aka— acceptance.

Acceptance can be as effective as forgiveness in relation to freeing yourself from the misdeeds of others, but it is not forgiveness. It doesn't carry the heavyweight punch of empowerment that comes with heartfelt forgiveness. Acceptance means that you have made a conscious decision to move beyond the offending issue and no longer let it affect you in the present moment. Meaning that you let the past be the past without having compulsive thoughts about revenge or unhealthy conversations in your head about the if's, whys, and what fors about the past wrongs.

I promised to give you an easy tool for practicing forgiveness, but let me say that if you find yourself not being able to go through the process I am going to teach you and fully reach a sense of peace or acceptance, meaning that there is no physical or emotional charge remaining around the issue, then please contact me, and I and will guide you through the process, or I will be able to direct you to someone who can.

It is important for you to read all the instructions prior to moving forward. It will be more beneficial to do this work after you have learned the techniques in the chapter on self-hypnosis.

<u>Find a comfortable place</u> - Someplace you can sit down, relax, and begin to focus your attention inward, possibly on your breathing or the beating of your heart, and relax until you are in a nice hypnotic trance, then start your work.

<u>Create a safe place in your mind -</u> A place where you are in control of everything. Make this space as grand as a palace room or as simple as a conference room, whatever works best for you is perfect.

<u>Create a seating area -</u> Some place within this safe space you will have a seating area with two chairs. Make one of the chairs powerful as if it is a throne of sorts, this will be your chair. Then make a smaller chair, one that strips power from whomever sits in it. Remember that in this place you have total control over everything, and nothing bad can happen to you here.

<u>Choose who you need to forgive -</u> This could be someone from the past or present. I suggest that you start with whoever first comes into your mind.

Recreate or imagine the offender and offense - As you do, watch what is happening as if it were happening on a tv or movie screen in front of you but not to you. Allow yourself to fully feel whatever feelings are coming up. If they are intense, allow them to be intense, get angry if you want to, and allow yourself to express those feelings in the next step.

Put the offender in the hot seat - With the offender in the smaller chair, unable to speak or move or do anything unless you say it's okay, tell them how their actions have impacted your life and how you feel about what they did to you. You can say whatever you want or need to say to them, and you keep going and get as expressive as you need to until you no longer feel angry, hurt, betrayed, or whatever it is. Once you have said what you need to say to them, move to the next step.

Check for residual feelings of anger or resentment - Take a deep breath and recall the offender and offense again and check to see how you feel. If you feel nothing, and I do not mean because of detachment or numbness of feeling, I mean you feel like you have gotten all that yucky angry energy expressed, then move forward.

Forgive – Remember, forgiveness is a gift you give yourself, it is not for the other person. The other person will never know they have been forgiven, and that is perfectly okay. It is now time for you to look at the offender who is sitting in the chair across from you and say to them, "I forgive you." Repeat this three more times, each time adding a reason why you forgive them. For example: "I forgive you because I want to be free of the pain you caused so that I can be a better mom, dad, partner, wife, husband."

Last check - Once you have forgiven, check inside again to make sure that you've cleared everything around this issue. Recall this issue again, and if you are free of any emotional or physical reaction, and your thoughts remain neutral in regard to the person, then you are free.

You will always come across people who are going to cross your boundaries and make you angry. You may even work with or live with someone who pushes your boundaries on a regular basis, and when that happens over and over again, you will either learn to accept them as they are without allowing things to bother you, or you will extricate yourself from the situation. If you can't extricate yourself because it is a rebellious child or ailing parent, then you need to practice automatic forgiveness. This is the process in which you are immediately able to forgive the offender because you know that if you are worth forgiving them once, then you are worth forgiving them again.

NLP Techniques

*It is hard to let old beliefs go. They are familiar. We are comfortable
with them and have spent years building systems and developing habits
that depend on them. Like a man who has worn eyeglasses so long that
he forgets he has them on, we forget that the world looks to us the way it
does because we have become used to seeing it that way through a
particular set of lenses. Today, however, we need new lenses.
And we need to throw the old ones away.*
— Kenichi Ohmae

First, what is NLP?

<u>Neuro:</u> Relating to the mind, and, more precisely, how
your state of mind affects your communication and behavior.
NLP provides a way to look at the state of mind and body to

70

allow you to build a mental map of your internal world, allowing you to see what is happening and, more importantly, how to make changes.

Linguistic: Relating to language and how our states of mind are demonstrated in our verbal and nonverbal communication. This allow us to gain access to what is happening internally and provides us with information that we may not have had or been unaware of.

Programming: Relating to your own internal programming like your beliefs, traditions, habitual thoughts, feelings, and even your reactions to certain stimuli, aka autopilot or cognitive fusion.

NLP is closely associated with hypnosis and offers many different techniques and methods of creating change in behavior patterns. I am going to teach you 4 of my favorite NLP techniques.

This first practice is called the *Circle of Power and Success.* It is a way to harness powerful positive energy and emotional states from past experiences and use them whenever you need to. (For an even more powerful experience, practice building the circle while in a state of self-hypnosis.)

Find a comfortable place where you can sit down and close your eyes. Take a deep breath and let all your thoughts go. Just sit there for a moment, breathe and let your mind wander, let all your troubles disappear.

Once you are relaxed, you will create an imaginary circle on the floor in front of you or in your mind's eye large enough for you to stand in. You can even imagine a bubble large enough for you to stand inside.

Now, search your memory for a time when you were young and experienced an amazing win. The one that brings a big smile to your face, makes you feel proud, and when you remember it, your shoulders get a little straighter, and you feel good about yourself. It could be as simple as getting an A on a test, getting 1st prize at the science fair, or maybe you had the winning heifer at the county fair, it really doesn't matter, you just need to recall a time when you were young and felt awesome about yourself or something you accomplished.

Build that positive energy up within yourself, remembering all the details of your past success, feeling what you felt, hearing what you heard, and seeing what you saw. Allow it to be as real for you today as it was when it happened. Allow yourself to smile and immerse yourself in the memory, and when you have built that energy as high as you can, enter the circle with all those powerful feelings and imagine as you do that, the space within the circle becomes alive with the color, or maybe the sounds and smells of your success. Stand in that circle feeling your power, hear it and see it.

Now, step out of the circle, leaving those powerful feelings alive within the circle, contained behind a forcefield of self-love and self-regard. Look inside that circle and see how alive it is with your powerful truth.

Notice when you step outside of the circle, your feelings return to neutral, and then step back into the circle, allowing the color or sound to immediately saturate you with those feelings of success again. This time see if you can build it up even more.

Breath it all in, enjoy it for a moment, and then as you exhale, step back out of the circle, leaving the power reserve behind.

Now, relax, and this time, search your memory for a time when you experienced success involving a skill. Recognize that this could mean a lot of different things, so whatever success involving a skill first comes into your thoughts is the perfect one to use because it is the one that your subconscious has chosen for you. Recall all you can about that success and allow yourself to feel all those good feelings, and just like the time before, intensify those feelings, making it as if it is happening again. See, hear, and feel the power behind your success, and step into the circle, bringing with you all those new resources, adding it to the swirl of powerful positive energy already flowing within it.

Notice that when you mix these two powerful states and resources how you feel. Allow the energy from inside the circle to fill you up, making you feel even more powerful and ready to take on anything. Stand there in your circle just enjoying how good it feels to be confident, powerful, and in control.

Now, step out of the circle, leaving those powerful feelings alive within the circle, contained behind a forcefield of self-love and self-regard. Look inside that circle and see how alive it is with your powerful truth.

Notice when you step outside of the circle, your feelings return to neutral, and then step back into the circle, allowing the color or sound to immediately saturate you with those feelings of success again. This time see if you can build it up even more. Breath it all in, enjoy it for a moment, and then, as you exhale, step back out of the circle, leaving the power reserve behind.

Now, let's apply this state to a future event. Choose an event that you have coming up in the future when you will want to enact this powerful resource state and feelings unconsciously. What is happening just before you want to have these feelings of success from the circle return again? Maybe it's when you see your office door, or when you put on the clothes you bought for the occasion or when you are introduced at a speaking engagement.

As you bring those cues to mind, step back into your circle and allow those feelings of success to come rushing back. Now imagine that future event unfolding, and as it does, recognize how all of your feelings of success are available to you. Recognize how you feel powerful and in control.

Now step out of the circle, leaving those powerful feelings alive within the circle, contained behind a forcefield of self-love and self-regard. Look inside that circle and see how alive it is with your powerful truth. How you have done that thing exactly right, for you.

When you have stepped out of the circle, reimagine the event and notice that you automatically recall the feelings of success, power, and confidence. This means that you have changed your mindset to one of success for your future event, and when it does arrive, your subconscious will automatically release that powerful state based on those cues you set.

Enjoy!

This next technique is called *Clarifying Internal Voices* and is a simplified version from the book *More Transforming Negative Self Talk* by Steve Andreas and is available on Amazon. I learned this simplified method from his son Mark Andres who possesses formidable skills and is a leader in the field.

This tool is used to clarify and transform the negative voices in your head into useful inner allies. It may be difficult to believe that such a thing is possible, even with voices that tell you that you're lazy, worthless, not good enough, or some other negative quality not printable here. When these voices start up, they can lead us down an ugly, dirty road filled with self-doubt and subsequent failure, and this is true even if we try not to listen to them! It turns out that clarifying and transforming a voice is much easier than trying to ignore or get rid of it, and, not only that, it leaves you with additional valuable resources that you'd be missing out on otherwise.

1. Select a voice – Remember a troublesome internal voice that has criticized your behavior in the present moment, reminded you of past failures or embarrassment, or foretold future failure, etc.

2. Listen to The Voice – Now, listen carefully to the sound of this voice—the tonality, volume, tempo, hesitations, etc. that you hear—all the qualities that allow you to recognize someone's voice on the phone instantly out of all of the thousands of voices you have heard.

3. Identify the voice – Whose voice is this? Is it your voice or someone else's? If it is someone else's voice, go directly to step 4, below. If it is not, ask, "Who did you learn from to talk in this way?" If you can't

identify the voice, ask if you did know, who would it be? Or who does this voice remind you of?

4. Add an image of the person – As you hear this voice, see the person who is speaking to you and watch all of their facial movements, expressions, gestures, etc. to find out what else you can learn about their experience as they talk to you.

5. Put it in a larger context – Now, expand the scope of what you see and hear to include the larger context in both space and time. Where are you, and what just happened that this person is responding to? View this event in detail, including what happened earlier that was relevant to this event, and also what happened later as a result, in order to understand it more fully and completely.

6. Notice the speaker's limitations – Notice what that person was simply unable to do because of their upbringing, beliefs, frustrations, or other inadequacies or limitations. Realize that both what they said and how they said it may have had very little to do with you and a great deal to do with their difficulty in communicating clearly and directly.

7. Clarify the message – Ask the person, "Would you please clarify your message? What would you say to me if you had been able to express yourself fully and speak honestly about all your experiences of this situation? What is it that you really want me to hear?"

8. <u>Give thanks for any clarification</u> – Thank this person for clarifying their communication. If the communication is still unclear, ask again—as many times as necessary, thanking them for each response —until their communication is clear to you.

9. <u>Ask for the positive intent</u> – Ask the person, "What is your positive intent in telling me this?" If the response doesn't appear to be positive, ask for the intent of this intent. Thank the person for this response and ask them, "What is your positive intent in telling me that?" You may need to ask several times before you receive an answer that you think is positive and that you can agree with. Usually, the positive intent is some kind of protection, either for you, the voice, a third person, or a group.

10. <u>Give sincere thanks for the positive intent</u> – Tell this person, "thanks very much for telling me your positive intent." Then ask them, "Would you be willing to consider communicating in a different way so that it would be much easier for me to pay full attention to what it is that you want me to hear?" Usually, you will get a "yes" answer, because this proposed change supports the positive intent in communicating with you even better than what it had been doing. If you get a "no" answer, that means that there has been some miscommunication. Back up one more step and clarify the miscommunication before moving forward again.

11. Explore different ways of communicating – Explore with this person different ways that they could speak to you until you find one that both of you like. This could mean different words, different voice tone, tempo, tonality, etc. Whatever most clearly communicates the positive intent.

12. Test in the context where the voice used to speak in the old way – Ask this voice to practice communicating to you in this new way in the original context or contexts where it used to speak to you in the old way, and find out how it goes. If it goes well, ask "Does any part of me have any objection or concerns about any of the changes that have been made?" If you notice any objections or resistance, back up one more step to modify how or when the voice speaks to you, and then come forward again.

13. Rehearse in the future – Imagine future situations where this voice can support you by communicating to you in this new way. Step in and experience, now, what it will be like.

Working with objections: If any objections arise in any sensory modality feelings, images, words or sounds, first discover whether or not it is actually an objection, and then do whatever is necessary to satisfy it in order to reach an agreement and congruence.

There are three different fundamental ways to satisfy an objection:

A. Adjust the change so that it no longer interferes with one or more other important outcomes that you have. For example, choose the voice of a different, trusted friend, and find out if that works better for you.

B. Carefully contextualize the change so that it doesn't occur in any context in which it might interfere with some other important outcome. For example, this change may only be appropriate in your personal life, not in your professional life, where it could cause trouble.

C. Reframe or re-categorize the meaning of either the change or the objection to the change so that there is no longer any conflict between their outcomes. You object to have this person speaking using your friend's voice because you think you might lose track of reality. But, actually, it is a sign of your creativity and flexibility; crazy people are very rigid and uncreative. And as long as you don't tell anyone else about this voice, it won't concern them.

Another great and fun way to quiet those nasty negative naysayers in your head is by playing with the voice itself and turning it into what it really is—nonsense. For example, if that voice says something like, "You're not smart enough to apply for that job!" You will take those exact words, and you will repeat them, but as you speak the words, you are going to change the voice to let's say Daffy Duck or even Beavis or Butthead or whatever funny voice works for you, but recognize when you change the voice, it loses its power over you. Or you are going to use what I call the slow it down method. Again, you will repeat the negative statement, only this time, you will do it out loud, and you will use multiple repetitions like this, "Yoooooooou arrrrrrrrre nnnnnnoooooooot ssssmaaaaarrt eeeeeeenoooooouuugh toooooo aaaaaaaaaplllllly fooooooor thaaaaaat joooooooob."

Notice what happens to the speaker behind the voice as you apply these simple tools. Not only do they lose their power, but if you do this every time it happens, the speaker eventually gives up and fades away.

Last but not least in the NLP tools that I love, is content reframing. This is a great tool for when you are in the thick of it and those bad thoughts just keep coming. For example, if you have experienced a painful separation or breakup and you keep obsessing over all the ifs ands why's and wherefores which in no way benefit you and only serve to make you feel worse about yourself, stop and consciously interrupt the thought pattern and start to think about all the awesome stuff that comes from being single like the freedom to do what you want when you want, and now that the old baggage is gone, you have the opportunity for the potential of a healthy and mutually beneficial relationship developing with someone special.

Hypnosis & Self Hypnosis

You use hypnosis not as a cure but as a means of establishing
a favorable climate in which to learn.
— Milton H. Erickson

Hypnosis is a fantasist tool if you want to create lasting changes to your beliefs, habits, and self-esteem. It is amazing at helping one to release past trauma, naturally birth children, and can even be used as a surgical anesthesia. Hypnosis uses your ability to focus the attention of your mind to create a trance state wherein you are able to effect change on a subconscious level. Basically, the conscious mind is relaxed while the subconscious mind is engaged through story, truisms, and questions that provoke insight and lead to creative problem solving. Hypnoses is useful for uncovering what is behind your thoughts, actions, and beliefs. You usually know what your thoughts are but are often confused as to why you have them, hypnosis can help provide those answers.

The effectiveness of hypnosis has been proven in multiple studies, and results like the ones demonstrated are not uncommon.

- 90.6% Success Rate for Smoking Cessation Using Hypnosis - *University of Washington School of Medicine, Depts. of Anesthesiology and Rehabilitation Medicine, Int J Clin Exp Hypn. 2001 Jul;49(3):257-66. Barber J.*

- Hypnosis More Than Doubled Average Weight Loss - *Kirsch, Irving (1996). Hypnotic enhancement of cognitive-behavioral weight loss treatments--Another meta-reanalysis. Journal of Consulting and Clinical Psychology, 64 (3), 517-519.*

- Hypnosis Has a Reliable and Significant Impact on Acute and Chronic Pain - *Hypnosis and clinical pain. Patterson DR, Jensen MP, Department of Rehabilitation Medicine, University of Washington School of Medicine, Seattle, WA USA 98104 Psychol Bull. 2003 Jul;129(4):495-521.*

You may have the idea when you visit a hypnotherapist like me that there is nothing for you to do but sit and listen and that you will be a changed person in one session just because I tell you a whole bunch of really cool things about yourself while you are in trance. And that is true, to a degree. The degree to which it is true relies solely on you and what it is that you are wanting to achieve. Expectations can play a large role in the success of any endeavor, and creating unreasonable expectations need to be avoided because I want you to look at how long it has taken you to get where you are and be okay with the fact that it may take some time to undo the knot you've tied. Changing your life is simple, but it is not easy, and there is no magic bullet. Like I tell clients who come to quit smoking, it is up to them to remain tobacco free because I am not going to follow them around and make sure they don't smoke.

There are many different styles or approaches to hypnosis, and you may prefer one over the other. The traditional style, or what I refer to as the traditional style, has a more directive approach, and the language patterns used are more in line with giving directions for one to follow. If you are the type of person who likes to be told what to do and then do it, this traditional style is a great place for you to start. If you are more the type who wants to be given the overall picture and then make your own connections, then you would find more success with an Ericksonian or permissive approach. Then there is the covert type of work, or what is called conversational hypnosis. It is my favorite to use with most clients because it taps into the power of neuroplasticity and the recognition of change at a conscious level in the present moment, otherwise known as seeing the light bulb come on. If you are unfamiliar with neuroplasticity, it is the brain's ability to undergo biological changes ranging from the cellular level (i.e., individual neurons) all the way to large-scale changes involving cortical remapping. This style of hypnosis requires no formal trance, although, after a session with a skilled conversational hypnotists, you are often left feeling a bit dazed and confused, aware that something wonderful and unique has taken place but not sure how to put it into words. Many clients have said with a smile on their face that they know they have changed but they are not sure why or how it happened.

When it comes to choosing a hypnotist to work with, follow the guidelines I lay out in the chapter, *It's Okay to Ask for Help.*

Self-Work

If you choose to practice on your own, that is okay because all hypnosis is self-hypnosis. You should practice for at least 10 minutes per day. I suggest practicing in the morning as you are waking up before you get out of bed because your mind and body are already relaxed, so all you have to do is keep your eyes closed and start providing suggestions as simple as "Today will be a good day." If you are having a stressful day, take a break and find someplace where you can sit undisturbed for as little as 5 minutes and focus on what it is that you want, or on what you already have. Practicing gratitude during a hypnotic state is a powerful suggestion in itself.

Here are three different techniques for inducing self-hypnosis. I have provided three so you can find the one that works best for you. If you follow these instructions, you will be able to reach a nice level of hypnosis to achieve your goals.

All these techniques require the use of passive concentration, which is nothing more than passive attention to a specific task, as if you are watching an event unfold but not part of the event. For example, if you want to use passive concentration to create warmth in your hands, you need only focus or think about what your hands feel like when they are warm. Imagine what it feels like when you are holding a warm bowl of soup or remember a time when you held your hands over a campfire, just focus intently and imagine what that would feel like and eventually you will begin to feel the warmth in your hands, and the same is true for any sensation, like heaviness or lightness.

Next is your ability to imagine or pretend, basically to suspend disbelief. This mindset helps you experience your body relaxing and becoming deeply relaxed by sensing it and knowing that it is happening without conscious intervention from you or you attempting to make it happen. The more you try to make it happen, the less it will happen, so just allow it to happen, sense it, and you will eventually be able to drop into a state of relaxation and heaviness anywhere at any time, regardless of what is taking place around you.

You will experience moments when your mind will wander off to something totally different than what you are attempting to do, that's okay. When you recognize that your mind has wandered away, just smile to yourself and bring it back to what you are doing.

Giving yourself suggestions is easy and can be accomplished in several ways, but the simplest is to picture the outcome you desire in your mind's eye and focus on it intently. Passively focus on your results as if nothing else matters and notice every detail of the outcome. Notice what you look like, what you are wearing, how your hair is different or maybe the same. Put yourself into the outcome you want fully by filling in the details as much as you can. It can be something as simple as visualizing that you have a $10,000 balance in your checking account. See your checkbook ledger in your mind with the balance you want and notice how that feels inside, and just enjoy that feeling.

Another great way is to simply induce hypnosis and repeating your desired result. For example, you could use, "I am now and forever free from _____" (insert challenge or issue here) or, "I have the power and ability to _____" (insert desired outcome). The suggestion should always be stated in a positive way like above. You need to focus on what you want and leave behind what you don't want because either way, you will get more of whatever you focus on.

This first technique focuses your attention on your breath.

1.   Find a quiet place where you are comfortable and you can sit down, close your eyes, and begin to relax.

2.   You will be using belly breaths. A belly breath is a deep breath that fills the deepest parts or the lower lobes of your lungs, and when you inhale, neither the chest or the shoulders are elevated or expanded, instead, the belly is pushed out as if it is being filled with air. Make sure you breathe in through your nose and then slowly exhale through the mouth, pushing your belly as far back toward the spine as you can so that the lungs are fully deflated of expired oxygen.

3.   Breathe in slowly, expanding your belly, and then you will hold it for a count of 3.

4.   Slowly exhale through your nose, and as you do, focus on relaxing more deeply. Just allow your joints to get loose and heavy as if you are preparing for a

nap. You may find it helpful to visualize the joints expanding and relaxing with each breath.

5. Take another slow, deep breath through your nose. Make sure that you are breathing into your belly and that you expand it fully. Then hold it for a count of 3.

6. When you exhale, allow your shoulders to drop down and allow your neck and jaw to relax. When your jaw is relaxed, the tip of the tongue should be touching the palate just behind your two front teeth, and the top and bottom teeth are not touching.

7. Take another deep breath in and hold it for a count of 3.

8. Release your breath all the way out, allowing your whole body to relax into a deep state of comfort and ease. Imagine your whole body is loose, limp, light, and relaxed, as if you were asleep at night.

9. Now, you will lift one of your arms up just a little bit and then let it just plop down heavily into your lap as if it had no bones.

10. Again, lift the arm just a little and let it fall. Now, let it just stay relaxed.

11. This time, you will use only your imagination to lift that same arm. You will just imagine lifting the arm, but you won't actually lift it in reality, just use your imagination.

12. In your mind, lift the arm again, and as you exhale, imagine or pretend that you are dropping it again. Just let the whole arm go limp, loose, and relaxed when you exhale. Each time you do that, it will double your relaxation.

13. Continue to loosen your muscles with each breath and create a safe place in your mind where you can allow yourself to feel safe and at peace. It could be someplace in nature like a forest or near a river, or anyplace you like where you feel happy and at your best.

14. It is time to begin giving your self suggestions.

15. Bring yourself back by simply wanting to return to the present moment. Take a deep breath, and when you exhale, open your eyes.

The next technique is easy and uses three of your senses: hearing, seeing, and feeling.

1. Find a quiet place where you are comfortable and you can sit down, close your eyes, and begin to relax.

2. Start by noticing what is in front of you. Notice what it is that you see, the ambient light, the color and texture of the things you see. Look into each thing deeply, allowing yourself to relax a little more every time you exhale.

3. Now, shift your focus to what you hear around you. What is the loudest sound you can hear? What is

a sound that is not loud or soft? And what is the faintest sound that you can hear? Can you hear your breath as it enters your lungs?

4. Shift your attention again. This time: focus on what it is that you can feel. How does your body feel when you are relaxed like this? What do your sleeves feel like against the skin on your arms? What about the temperature of the air as it moves across your skin?

5. Repeat steps 2 - 4 three times, allowing yourself to go deeper and deeper into calmness and relaxation with each round.

6. Continue to loosen your muscles with each breath and create a safe place in your mind where you can allow yourself to feel safe and at peace. It could be someplace in nature like a forest or near a river or anyplace you like where you feel happy and at your best.

7. It is time to begin giving your self suggestions.

8. Bring yourself back by simply wanting to return to the present moment. Take a deep breath, and when you exhale, open your eyes.

The next technique is also very easy and very quick.

15. Find a quiet place where you are comfortable and you can sit down, close your eyes, and begin to relax.

1. Choose a spot on the wall or some object in front of you but slightly above your line of sight but not so far above it that you have to tilt your head.

2. Stare at that spot or object with such intensity it is as if there are laser beams shooting from your eyes onto that spot or object. Say the number 20 and close your eyes.

3. Keep your eyes fixated on your spot and continue counting backward while opening and closing your eyes with each number until you reach the number 1.

4. Continue to loosen your muscles with each breath and create a safe place in your mind where you can allow yourself to feel safe and at peace. It could be someplace in nature like a forest or near a river, or anyplace you like where you feel happy and at your best.

5. It is time to begin giving your self suggestions.

6. Bring yourself back by simply wanting to return to the present moment. Take a deep breath, and when you exhale, open your eyes.

You are sure to find one of these techniques useful in reaching your goals. Remember to practice at a minimum of 10 minutes per day.

For a free Hypnosis Relaxation MP3 and other resources visit excelhypnosis.com.

Basic EFT

"The expectations of life depend upon diligence; the mechanic that
would perfect his work must first sharpen his tools."
— Confucius

This chapter will introduce you to an extremely useful
tool called *Emotional Freedom Technique* or *Tapping*. Like most of
the ideas I have presented, I am going to provide you with the
basics, and then you decide if it is a technique you want to learn
more about.

Emotional Freedom Technique was developed by Gary Craig
and uses the same basic energetic pathways as acupressure and is
considered by many to be a form of energy medicine. Follow the
steps below, and you will get results, guaranteed.

I had a client who came to see me for weight loss, and on her intake, she indicated the she would often drive to her favorite local bakery and purchase multiple cakes and pastries and that she would consume them while sitting in her parked car. She admitted that at times, even the smell of chocolate would create such an intense craving that she would have to go to the store to purchase a cake, and she would then sit and eat the entire thing and then cry afterward. She had to lose 40 pounds in order to undergo knee replacement surgery but she couldn't find the strength to fight the cravings. The day arrived for her first session with me, and I prepared for her session by visiting the bakery across the street from my office and purchasing the most decadent slice of chocolate cake they had on display. They put the $12.00 slice of cake into a pretty pink box, and I headed back to my office excited to present this client with her biggest enemy.

She arrived, and we talked for a few moments, and then I excused myself and retrieved the cake from the refrigerator, and when I returned to the room and presented her with the chocolate filled pretty pink box, she looked at me like I was the stupidest person she had ever shared her issues with. She was, to say at the least, a bit flabbergasted that I was offering her the very thing that she wanted freedom from. I asked her to open the box and smell the cake and to even touch the cake. She reluctantly did as I asked, and I could see the change on her face as the scent lit up her olfactory center. I could even see that her mouth was getting wet as she began to swallow more. I asked her to rate her craving between 1 and 10. She said 20 and advised me that if she was alone, she would eat the cake right there and then. I then asked her to describe what she was feeling and thinking, and her only thoughts were on how good the cake smelled. Then I walked her through the EFT protocol and had her pick the box back up and smell the cake again. And again, I asked her to rate the level of craving she was experiencing between 1 and 10. This time, it was 0. That's right, ZERO. Her eyes were as big as a saucer as she kept smelling and smelling the cake, attempting to bring back up the craving with no success. I asked her if she wanted to take the cake home to enjoy later. "No" came out very quickly, and as she said it, she handed the box back to me. I do not believe that anything in life is all or nothing, unless you are an addict or alcoholic, because as I stated in an earlier chapter, what we resist persists. I believe that if you are in a state of emotional, spiritual, and physical balance, all things can be enjoyed. Again, that statement does not apply to heroine, cocaine, Hennessy, or most other stimulates, even cigarettes.

Here is the protocol as taught by Gary Craig. You can find more information about EFT by visiting emofree.com

First, become familiar with the specific points you'll be tapping on.

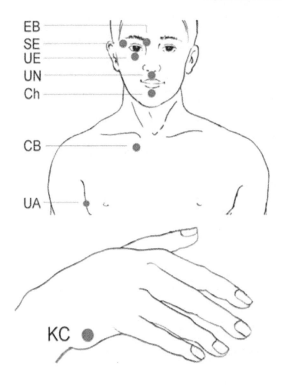

KC: The Karate Chop point (abbreviated KC) is located at the center of the fleshy part of the outside of your hand (either hand) between the top of the wrist and the base of the baby finger or... stated differently... the part of your hand you would use to deliver a karate chop.

TOH: On the top of the head. If you were to draw a line from one ear, over the head, to the other ear, and another line from your nose to the back of your neck, the TOH point is where those two lines would intersect.

EB: At the beginning of the eyebrow, just above and to one side of the nose. This point is abbreviated EB for beginning of the EyeBrow.

SE: On the bone bordering the outside corner of the eye. This point is abbreviated SE for Side of the Eye.

UE: On the bone under an eye about 1 inch below your pupil. This point is abbreviated UE for Under the Eye.

UN: On the small area between the bottom of your nose and the top of your upper lip. This point is abbreviated UN for Under the Nose.

Ch: Midway between the point of your chin and the bottom of your lower lip. Even though it is not directly on the point of the chin, we call it the chin point because it is descriptive enough for people to understand easily. This point is abbreviated Ch for Chin.

CB: The junction where the sternum (breastbone), collarbone and the first rib meet. To locate it, first place your forefinger on the U-shaped notch at the top of the breastbone (about where a man would knot his tie). From the bottom of the U, move your forefinger down toward the navel 1 inch and then go to the left (or right) 1 inch. This point is abbreviated CB for CollarBone even though it is not on the collarbone (or clavicle) per se. It is at the beginning of the collarbone and we call it the collarbone point because that is a lot easier to say than "the junction where the sternum (breastbone), collarbone, and the first rib meet."

UA: On the side of the body, at a point even with the nipple (for men) or in the middle of the bra strap (for women). It is about 4 inches below the armpit. This point is abbreviated UA for underarm.

The 5 Steps of The EFT Tapping Basic Protocol

1. All you do here is make a mental note of what ails you. This becomes the target at which you "aim" the EFT Tapping Basic Recipe. Examples might be: Sore shoulder, my father embarrassing me at my age 8 birthday party or hitting that high singing note. Be sure you are only targeting one issue at a time. As you will learn later, trying to combine issues in the process will compromise your results.

2. Test the initial Intensity: Here, you establish a before level of the issue's intensity by assigning a number to it on a 0-10 scale where 10 is the worst the issue has ever been and 0 is no problem whatsoever. This serves as a benchmark so we can compare our progress after each round of The EFT Tapping Basic Recipe. If, for example, we start at an 8 and eventually reach a 4, then we know we have achieved a 50% improvement. The number of possible issues we can address with The EFT Tapping Basic Recipe is endless, and they don't all fit into neat testing boxes. That is why we have an entire segment later on dedicated to Testing Your EFT Tapping Work. For this stage of your learning, however, here are some useful methods to help you access your issue(s) and arrive at your 0-10 numbers. They apply to most issues.

For emotional issues, you can recreate the memories in your mind and assess their discomforts.

For physical ailments, you can simply assess the existing pain or discomfort.

For performance issues, you can attempt the desired performance level and measure how close you come to it.

3. The Setup: The Setup is a process we use to start each round of Tapping. By designing a simple phrase and saying it while continuously Tapping the KC point, you let your system know what you're trying to address.

When designing this phrase there are two goals to achieve:

1) acknowledge the problem

2) accept yourself in spite of it

We do this by saying:

"Even though I have this _____, I deeply and completely accept myself."

The blank above represents the problem you want to address, so you can just insert things like:

This sore shoulder: "Even though I have this sore shoulder, I deeply and completely accept myself."

This fear of spiders: "Even though I have this fear of spiders, I deeply and completely accept myself."

This humiliation at my eighth-grade graduation: "Even though I have this humiliation at my eighth grade graduation, I deeply and completely accept myself."

This difficulty making free throws: "Even though I have this difficulty making free throws, I deeply and completely accept myself."

Not all of the issues will fit neatly into "Even though I have this _____," so you can use some flexibility when designing your Setup phrase. For example, instead of "this sore shoulder" you could say, "Even though my shoulder hurts, I deeply and completely accept myself." Or instead of "this humiliation at my eighth grade graduation" you could say, "Even though my dad humiliated me at my eighth grade graduation."

By using "Even though I have this _____," you will automatically choose something that represents your experience, your reaction, or a problem that you recognize as something that belongs to you, and that is an important feature.

We do not want to use EFT on someone else's problem. For example, rather than, "Even though my son is addicted to drugs, I deeply and completely accept myself," it's better to focus on your own reaction, which might be, "Even though I'm frustrated by my son's drug addiction." Or instead of "Even though my husband works too much…," better to try something like, "Even though I feel alone when my husband stays late at the office…" We want to aim EFT at our part of the problem rather than trying to fix someone else's problem.

By identifying the problem with this phrase, you "set up" the initial energy disruption behind the scenes so the Tapping has something to resolve.

Important, Important, Important:

The language that we use always aims at the negative. This is essential because it is the negative that creates the energy disruptions that The EFT Tapping Basic Recipe clears (and thus brings peace to the system). By contrast, conventional methods and popular self-help books stress positive thinking and preach avoiding the negative. This sounds good but, for our purposes, it does little more than cover over the negative with pleasant sounding words. EFT, on the other hand, needs to aim at the negative so it can be neutralized. This allows our natural positives to bubble up to the top.

4. The Sequence: This is the workhorse part of The EFT Tapping Basic Recipe that stimulates/balances the body's energy pathways. To perform it, you tap each of the points shown in the Sequence Points diagram (see above) while saying a Reminder Phrase that keeps your system tuned into the issue. I list the points below followed by a description of the Reminder Phrase:

Top of the Head (TOH)

Beginning of the Eyebrow (EB)

Side of the Eye (SE)

Under the Eye (UE)

Under the Nose (UN)

Chin Point (CH)

Beginning of the Collarbone (CB)

Under the Arm (UA)

The Reminder Phrase is quite simple, as you need only identify the issue with some brief wording. Depending on your issue, you might say the following at each tapping point....

"This sore shoulder",

"My father embarrassed me",

"This difficulty in singing that high note."

5. Test the Intensity Again: Finally, you establish an "after" level of the issue's intensity by assigning a number to it on a 0-10 scale. You compare this with the before level to see how much progress you have made. If you are not down to zero, then repeat the process until you either achieve zero or plateau at some level.

Again, this is only touching the surface of what EFT can provide. If this tool resonates with you, then I suggest looking further into his techniques and exploring "The Unseen Therapist" free intro e-book. https://www.emofree.com/ unseen-therapist/ read-this-first.html

100

It is OKAY to Ask for Help

"Regardless of what challenge you are facing right now, know that it has not come to stay. It has come to pass. During these times, do what you can with what you have, and ask for help if needed. Most importantly, never surrender. Put things in perspective. Take care of yourself. Find ways to replenish your energy, strengthen your faith and fortify yourself from the inside out."
— Les Brown

Why is it so hard to ask for help? Because you don't want to feel vulnerable. You have been taught to feel ashamed of needing that kind of help. Basically, just ways to trick yourself and keep yourself shielded from reality. An excuse for what you call being stuck.

Imagine driving down a two-lane country road late at night in the howling wind and rain. Suddenly, a deer appears in your headlights, and in an attempt to avoid the deer, you crash into a deep muddy ditch. Do you abandon the car because you are too embarrassed to tell someone you didn't want to kill poor Bambi? Do you attempt to get it out of the ditch yourself, refusing help? Or, do you look for someone who can help pull you out of the ditch so that you can get on with your life? Sounds like a no brainer, right? Unfortunately, when that vehicle is your life, and the deer is the breakup of a relationship that sends into you into that ditch, not only do you refuse to ask for help, you probably won't even take your foot off the gas.

Stop!

Like everything in life, you have choices when it comes to asking for help, and I am going to introduce you to the ones that I have seen the greatest results with.

The easiest and most cost-effective way to get help is find a CoDA meeting, aka Co-Dependents Anonymous meeting. I can hear it now, "Oh, geez, an anonymous meeting, really?" That may be your reaction, or maybe you have already found a degree of recovery from alcohol, overeating, financial issues, or any other of a number of things in an organized 12 step program. If your initial response includes resistance to the idea of going to a 12-step meeting, then you need to go to a 12-step meeting. They are safe, and by you attending, even if you don't participate in the sharing portion, you are providing support for the recovery of those who do share.

I suggest CoDA because if you are dealing with anger, control issues, low self-esteem, lack of self-worth and/or

102

unhealthy relationships, then you are ultimately dealing with some degree of codependency.

Here is an excerpt from the "Am I Co Dependent?" pamphlet.

Denial Patterns

Codependents often...

1. have difficulty identifying what they are feeling.

2. minimize, alter, or deny how they truly feel.

3. perceive themselves as completely unselfish and dedicated to the well-being of others.

Low Self-esteem Patterns

Codependents often....

1. have difficulty making decisions.

2. judge what they think, say, or do harshly, as never good enough.

3. are embarrassed to receive recognition, praise, or gifts.

4. are unable to identify or ask for what they need and want.

5. value others' approval of their thinking, feelings, and behavior over their own.

6. do not perceive themselves as lovable or worthwhile persons.

Compliance Patterns

Codependents often....

1. compromise their values and integrity to avoid rejection and other people's anger.

2. are very sensitive to other's feelings and assume the same feelings.

3. are extremely loyal, remaining in harmful situations too long.

4. place a higher value on other's opinions and feelings and are afraid to express differing viewpoints or feelings.

5. put aside their own interests in order to do what others want.

6. accept sex as a substitute for love.

Control Patterns

Codependents often...

1. believe people are incapable of taking care of themselves.

2. attempt to convince others what to think, do, or feel.

3. become resentful when others decline their help or reject their advice.

4. freely offer advice and direction without being asked.

5. lavish gifts and favors on those they want to influence.

6. use sex to gain approval and acceptance.

7. have to feel needed in order to have a relationship with others.

Avoidance Patterns

Codependents often...

1. act in ways that invite others to reject, shame, or express anger toward them.

2. judge harshly what others think, say, or do.

3. avoid emotional, physical, or sexual intimacy to avoid feeling vulnerable.

4. allow addictions to people, places, and things to distract them from achieving intimacy in relationships.

5. use indirect or evasive communication to avoid conflict or confrontation.

6. believe displays of emotion are a sign of weakness.

Note: a longer list of patterns and characteristics is available in other pieces of CoDA literature and online at coda.org

What you need to keep in mind is that when you go to a meeting like CoDa, you are going to hear your story coming out of someone else's mouth. It will humble you in ways that you have never experienced. To finally know someone who undoubtedly knows your story because in their sharing of experience, strength, and hope, you saw your childhood and your mother or maybe your current relationship. It can be the most sobering and rewarding hour of your week. The only trick to recovery through CoDA alone is finding a good healthy meeting with lots of recovery in the room, meaning that at least some of the members in the group have multiple years of working the program and have guided others through the12 steps of the program. You will make friends, and you will find a real sense of community as you start to open up and allow your healing to begin. Once you are in the program long enough, sponsor a new member and experience growth and healing in ways you never thought possible.

The one area I disagree with when it comes to 12-Step programs is the belief that once a codependent always a codependent or the idea that you will never fully escape its grasp. To that, I say, "BS." I will not allow any organization or person to tell me who I am or what I can or cannot recover from. When I attend meetings now, I upset people because I will not say, "Hello my name is Anthony and I am a codependent." Instead I say, "Hi my name is Anthony and I used to suffer from codependency." When asked about this, I simply tell them that as a person who helps others heal through the use of language patterns, I do not believe it is healthy to re-enforce a negative self-image, and that by essentially saying that you are something, you are creating more of it. If I keep telling everyone I am that, how can I be something different? In other words, if you want to change your story, you need to start telling a new one.

If a meeting will not work for you, then you will want to look for a professional who understands you and the challenges you are facing. If money is the first thing you consider, then buck up and go to a CoDA meeting. They are free! Otherwise, expect to pay a fair price. I am not saying that expensive means better, what I am saying is that you should not choose who you are going to work with based on price alone.

Here are the top 4 things to consider when choosing the best professional guide for your journey.

1. Do you believe they can help you? This is one of the most important questions, and the answer can only be found by looking within. This is when you put your head, your heart, and your intuition to work simultaneously. When you are comfortable with the logical considerations like licensure, training, and insurance, then check your heart. When speaking with the perspective guide, do they make you feel good and inspire you? If the answer is yes, the final check comes from your intuition. This is a sense or a feeling that you have that says, "Yes, I feel good about this." This is the trifecta of decision making, and when done in earnest, the results will not lead you astray.

2. How much training do they have? This is where things can get tricky. Each state, and in some cases, each county in a state, have their own governing laws for the type of training one needs in order to practice in the field of mental health. Some states require the

practitioner to be, at minimum, a licensed clinical social worker, and in some states, there is no requirement beyond a high school education. The amount of college education in western psychology and diagnosis' is not as important as the ability to understand where you are in your process and how best to guide you to where you want to be. You should consider what you are wanting to overcome or change and allow that to be a guide. If you are seeking relief from chronic pain, make sure that the person has been certified in a pain management protocol or has experience with recovery from chronic pain. If you seek freedom from tobacco, seek out a certified tobacco cessation specialist or someone with experience in addictions. The real gift is finding someone who is trained in a multitude of techniques, because that person can usually offer an approach that is more tailored to your needs. When it comes to training, look for someone who has done research into the healthy human condition, philosophy, world religions, the human body, codependency, addictions, the mind-body connection, and consciousness. The more well-rounded your guide is, the better you will be served.

3. How successful are the clients they work with at achieving their goals? This is a doozy of a question and is so multifaceted that it definitely needs to be addressed. Unrealistic expectations can be avoided when you understand that in order for you to be successful at any level, you must really want to make the change for yourself. You are not doing it to shut

up the nagging wife, husband, kids, or grandkids. You are not doing it because the doctor says so or because of peer pressure. In order for you to be successful, you have to really want to change. You have to be doing it because you want to do it. Even though your success rate is largely dependent on your desire to be successful, there is also the responsibility of your guide or teacher to be considered, after all, it takes two to tango. It is their job to provide you with a safe environment that encourages growth through introspection, forgiveness, and acceptance or whatever tools or theories need to be employed to help you be successful. Guiding change work is very much a dance between those involved, there is an ebb and flow that must be honored. It is like a dance teacher and the student they work with. The teacher can instruct the student in the proper technique and movements, but it is up to the student to make those movements into something beautiful.

4. Have they done their own work? A controversial question for sure. It is, again, important to find these sorts of things out. For example, would it be a good idea to see someone for relationship issues if you have seen them being disrespectful to their own partner or coworkers? Should an alcoholic seek help from someone who is also in the throes of alcoholism? It is not reasonable to expect anyone to be perfect or beyond life's challenges. It is reasonable, however, to expect the person who is guiding you to be on their own path of continual improvement and growth. When you interview them, get a sense for

how open they are to share some of the experiences that have shaped them and moved them toward what they do in helping others. Are they willing to be open about how they have triumphed over challenges?

You are worth asking for help, and, trust me on this point, no one will think bad of you for it.

Putting It All Together

"Learning isn't a means to an end; it is an end in itself."
— *Robert A. Heinlein*

Now it is time to start to implement some of the techniques you have learned, and a great way to keep track of your progress is by keeping a journal. I know some folks are reluctant to spend the time journaling, and if you are one of them, I want you to put aside your aversion and take the time, because if your happiness and success is important enough for you to have read this book, then I implore you to please continue investing your time and energy so that you can reach your full potential. No one else will, and it is not their responsibility.

If you don't know where to start when it comes to journaling, that's okay because I am going to provide you with several journaling activities, and the first one is so simple that anyone can do it.

Start a daily gratitude list. You will write down a minimum of 10 things that you are grateful for each night before you go to bed. This activity is simple and will not take up a bunch of your time. The benefits of doing this will not show up overnight. Instead, they reveal themselves over time as the list gets bigger and easier to fill in, and then you'll start to notice that those negative ways of thinking move to the side and positive thoughts start to rule your world.

The next activity will take some thought because you will be answering questions that on the surface seem pretty straight forward, but when you start to dive into them, they are anything but surface quality. The questions will help you to formulate suggestions while practicing self-hypnosis and will help you understand your unconscious motives as well as barriers. As you answer them, notice what you feel and if negative thoughtforms show up.

For example: Let's say that you want to stop working for other people and become self-employed. You'd write something like, I want to be successful self-employed. Did that voice pop up and stat to give you all the reasons why that can't happen? Here is where you need to really pay attention to internal voices, because if that is what you want but that voice in your head says you can't do it because you're too old, or you don't have enough money saved up in case it doesn't work, or whatever the voice says that negates the idea, you need to learn to question it immediately by using the *Clarifying Internal Voices* process that you learned earlier.

1. What do you really want? (Pay attention to any negative messaging you may receive.)

2. What does that look like? (Be specific, imagine every detail of whatever it is that you want. From the example above, you would write down in detail what your work space looks like and who your clients are and how much you charge them for your services, everything that describes what it is that you want.)

3. What will having that do for you specifically? (Will having it help you to get that new car? Or maybe it will provide you the opportunity to get paid while you travel the world.)

4. How will you know when you've got it? (What will be different in your life that shows you that you have whatever it is? From the example above, you could write, "I'll know I have it because my schedule is full of new clients."

5. What has stopped you from having it until now? (Write down all the things that have stopped you from getting it in the past. For example, "I am afraid I won't be able to pay my bills, or I won't be able to afford to pay for my family's health insurance.")

6. How will having or achieving that affect the people around you? (This is doozy! Why? Because as much as you distress the people around you with your

unhealthy behavior at times, they may become irritated or troubled that you are changing, because that means that they will have to interact with you in new ways that may be outside of their own comfort zones. If you are involved in a bad relationship, and you start to change, the person you are involved with will become fearful because they will need to change in order to remain a part of your new healthy way of being, and it will be your job to hold the line and stay true to your wants and desires, even if it means cutting unhealthy people out of your life.)

It is now time for you to set yourself free and begin to live the life you were meant to live when you came into this world. And because you now have these tools, you will be able to achieve any goal you set.

Let's have a short review here of what you have learned. Because I showed you:

> A. some of the basic truths about who you really are, you will be able to more easily recognize your strengths and value.

> B. how to use your mind instead of your mind using you, you will be able to recognize when you are sabotaging your life and dreams.

> C. how your energetic system works, you have a better way to understand the types of energetic patterns that drive your unconscious behavior.

D. how to surrender, you will have much more influence over things that are out of your immediate control.

E. how to forgive others and yourself, you are free from the ugly stuff from the past that kept you angry and stuck and kept you from being who you really are and living the life you really want.

F. how to use the NLP technique for the Circle of Power and Success, you will be able to trigger a mindset of success at any time.

G. how to use self-hypnosis, you will be able to motivate yourself and keep yourself on a positive path toward success and freedom from whatever ails you.

H. how to use EFT, you have total control over cravings, intense emotional states, and even some physical discomfort.

You are on your way to a new and rewarding way of living your life, and I want you to enjoy the journey. Remember, there will be times when you take 2 steps forward and 3 backward, IT'S OKAY! Give yourself a break, it takes time to relearn and implement change, and no one can do it overnight. After all, you did not get to where you are overnight.

If you are interested in additional training or working with me, please visit excelhypnosis.com or send me an email, anthony@exelhypnosis.com.

Thank you and best wishes.

Appendix

Invictus

by William Ernest Henley

Out of the night that covers me,

   Black as the Pit from pole to pole,

I thank whatever gods may be

   For my unconquerable soul.

In the fell clutch of circumstance

   I have not winced nor cried aloud.

Under the bludgeonings of chance

   My head is bloody, but unbowed.

Beyond this place of wrath and tears

Looms but the Horror of the shade,

And yet the menace of the years

Finds, and shall find, me unafraid.

It matters not how strait the gate,

How charged with punishments the scroll.

I am the master of my fate:

I am the captain of my soul.

For more information about EFT visit "The Unseen Therapist" free intro e-book. https://www.emofree.com/unseen-therapist/read-this-first.html

For more information about Carolyn Myss, Archetypes and Scared Contracts visit: https://www.myss.com

For more information about Mark Andreas and NLP visit: For more information visit markandreas.com.

Made in the USA
Middletown, DE
03 June 2022

66624827R00070